M000032215

BE BRILLIANT!

How to Master the Sales Skill of
Persuasive Questioning

Scott O. Baird, Ph.D.

6TH DIMENSION PRESS
UTAH

6th Dimension Press
2066 South 950 East
Provo, UT 84606

ISBN 978-1-947248-00-7

Printed in the United States of America

For More Information About
Be Brilliant! Books & Training for Teams & Leaders
801-225-7000
www.GriffinHill.com

To my dad, Frederick T. Baird 1924-2017

He taught me by example to
  Work hard
  Have integrity
  Sincerely care about your customer
  When you sell, be brilliant! And you will prosper.

ACKNOWLEDGEMENTS

Over the years, loyal clients and good friends have encouraged me to capture the Griffin Hill Sales System in book form. My own writing phobia and the monumental weight of doing justice to such an important subject fueled procrastination and excuses. Even now, I would like more time to augment, refine, and polish before I publish. Perhaps that feeling never goes away—no matter how much polish is applied. So, my dear friends and loyal clients, thank you for your encouragement. *Be Brilliant!* is not the full Griffin Hill Sales System in book form, but it represents an important start.

In the course of our study into sales and selling, we tracked behavioral data of more than 3,500 salespeople. A like number participated in regular coaching sessions without recording their data. This contribution from more than 7,000 salespeople, leaders, marketers, entrepreneurs, and business owners was a tremendous influence in the writing of this book. Their insight, feedback, advocacy, and use of the Griffin Hill Sales System helped shape what all of us at Griffin Hill believe to be the most powerful system of sales available today. Thanks to them for their valuable contribution.

Because my name is on the cover, I am responsible for the content of *Be Brilliant.* Though I accept full responsibility, it is only by the hard work of many other people that this book became a reality. The contribution of Todd Burnham is especially noteworthy. His editorial influence made the book more enjoyable to read. His unrivaled ability to add clarity to the written word using graphical presentation is a wonderful contribution to this book. I am grateful for his collaborative influence.

Finally, a big thanks to Cameron Baird who is brilliant in his leadership of Griffin Hill, the performance company I founded more than 30 years ago. His leadership enables me to research, write and engage our customers. No father could hope for a better son.

CONTENTS

SECTION I

LAYING THE GROUNDWORK

Be Brilliant!

Chapter One

The Griffin Hill Sales System:
Background and Introduction

Griffin Hill, the human and organizational performance firm that I founded more than 30 years ago, has been doing sales research for more than a decade. This research has resulted in a proven method for sales success. Our research study has included companies with a nationwide profile like Xerox, Lexus Nexus, InsideSales.com, Legal Zoom, Vivant and iHeart Media. It also included companies with a more regional influence like Moreton and Company, A Plus Benefits and RBM Building Services. Our research would not be complete (would not have integrity) if we hadn't included smaller companies that sell a variety of products and services in their local market, including pest control, insurance, advertising, software development, computer maintenance, wealth creation advisories, and light manufacturing.

IntegraCore is one example of Griffin Hill efficacy. When we first began coaching IntegraCore they had less than two million in annual revenue.

Using the Griffin Hill Sales System, they grew revenue by more than 200% per year for 6 years in a row.

IntegraCore Annual Revenue

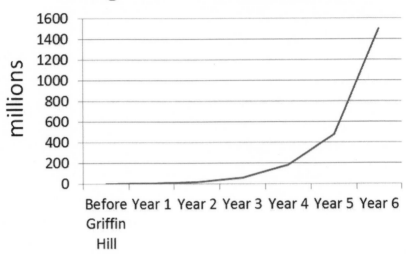

Their overall growth of more than 2000% during those years landed them on Inc.'s fastest growing companies list and eventually boosted them into the Inc. 5000 list. Founders and owners of IntegraCore salute Griffin Hill and our sales system as a significant contributor to that growth and success.

Our research is ongoing. So far, to date, it includes more than 3,500 salespeople, in excess of 144,000 sales cases and over 467,000 sales interactions. The lessons learned have shaped and built the Griffin Hill Sales System.

A system, like a building or a ship's hull should be whole, complete, without gap or flaw. It should have structural integrity. Additionally, it should stimulate honesty in every interaction. The Griffin Hill Sales System is built on principles of respect, fidelity and honesty.

One important part of the Griffin Hill Sales System is the Needs Audit Routine.

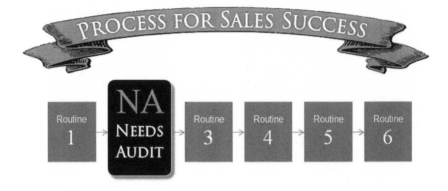

The Needs Audit is a discovery process for the salesperson and for the buyer. The Needs Audit is where persuasion really happens. It is the exclusive domain of successful salespeople. Mastery of the principles and techniques of the Needs Audit Routine is essential for professionals who aspire to be among the top 1% of sales performers. Because the Needs Audit is so important in the development of a professional salesperson, it is broken out for separate, in-depth instruction in this book. If you seek sales mastery and the financial rewards that accompany it, this book is an essential read. It should be in the reference library of every salesperson and entrepreneur.

The Needs Audit has unrivaled capacity to produce persuasive power and to build a revenue generating engine. This capacity to produce power and revenue is in the ability of the Needs Audit to guide salespeople, entrepreneurs and business people to create and use brilliant questions.

Chapter Two

Seek First to Understand

When You Understand Your Suspects, Prospects, and Buyers, It Will Transform Your Personal Economy

Human beings are a tumble of emotions and motivations. The complexity of influences can be difficult to sort out and organize. Sometimes we don't even understand ourselves, let alone the conditions and cares that trigger decision and action in others. When the bright light of mutual understanding sparks, however, all things are possible for salesperson and buyer. Suddenly the future looks bright. Hope springs to mind and heart. Opportunity becomes reality. Buyers escape pain. Salespeople win deals, generate revenue and earn commissions.

> **When the bright light of mutual understanding sparks, all things are possible for salesperson and buyer.**

The ability to stimulate discovery and create mutual understanding is a unique and rare gift. The amazing truth is that this gift can be learned, cultivated, practiced and mastered.

Mastery brings transformation. The transformed master is respected as an elite professional whose skill is in high demand and for which the master is well compensated. This book will begin the journey of transformation professionally and economically.

If You Must Speak, Ask a Question

I was scanning the newspaper for articles of interest when I saw a headline that did its job. It grabbed my attention and I read the Boyd Matheson op ed piece he wrote for the Deseret News in Salt Lake City[1]. That headline, "If You Must Speak, Ask a Question," captured the wisdom of the ages. More than just a headline, it is a call to action that every salesperson should heed. If you want to be an elite performer, internalize that message. Asking questions is fundamental to persuasion. Not only do good questions help you to understand your potential buyer—brilliant questions stimulate discovery of need and want for what you are selling in the mind and heart of the buyer. Though Matheson was not speaking to or about salespeople— he was speaking of society in general, his article suggests that the twin skills of asking questions and listening to others are the dying art of genteel social interaction.

Matheson explained, "The skills that bring about dynamic conversations and elevated interactions—listening and asking questions—are nearly extinct."

That is sage thinking that every salesperson hoping to master their craft and rise in their profession should understand. Salespeople should hope for and aim for *dynamic conversations and elevated interactions.* That is the type of exchange that earns you the status of "trusted advisor."

"You can do far more with a question than you can ever do with a statement," says Matheson.

"By asking a question you are showing you are interested… The natural byproduct of asking a question is that the other person will be more open and more likely to listen to you."

Kudos to you, Mr. Matheson! Your assertions are right on point. They lay the foundation for our discussion as we explore the social and scientific underpinnings of the truth contained in this book.

Summary: Seek First to Understand

Dr. Stephen R. Covey authored the landmark book, "The 7 Habits of Highly Effective People." Dr. Covey's 5th habit is "seek first to understand, then to be understood." Certainly, questions can help you, the salesperson, in your quest for understanding. Dr. Covey's 5th habit goes beyond questions, it requires listening. Listening does not mean just being quiet while the buyer speaks. Listening isn't jumping in to the conversation with your own story or experience, even if your intent is to show empathy.

Listening isn't contemplating your next response or question while the buyer speaks. Listening is the sincere intent to understand your buyer's thoughts, feelings and motives. Asking questions is important. Asking the right questions is crucial. Asking questions that illuminate understanding is brilliant!

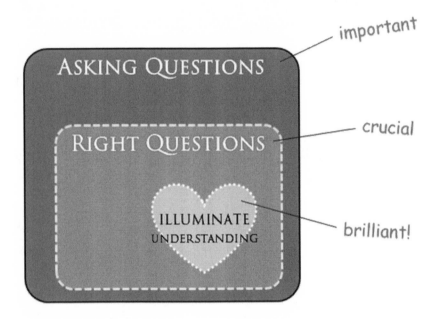

Chapter Three

The Majesty of Brilliant Questions

Asking Brilliant Questions Is the Mark of Uncommon Salesmanship

If asking questions and listening that promote mutual understanding are becoming extinct in the general population, they are most certainly the dinosaurs of a long past era in sales circles. Too often, glibness of tongue and jocular non-stop talking that passes for wit, are the most valued attributes by those recruiting salespeople.

In the competitive sea of poorly trained salespeople, the master of brilliant questions, one with the skill to really listen, is as uncommon as teeth in a laying hen. Such a skill stacks the odds of success in favor of the skilled and professional salesperson.

Brilliant Questions Illuminate the Path

A question is 'brilliant' when it illuminates understanding. For a salesperson, understanding what is important to the buyer is essential but not the full extent of the power of brilliant questions.

Brilliant questions should also stimulate new discovery of understanding in the buyer. By shining the light of understanding on critical buyer needs, brilliant questions can help the buyer to see conditions or situations that have been neglected, overlooked, or unconsidered. Finally, Brilliant questions shine the light of understanding on the seller's value proposition. In this way, brilliant questions help the buyer to discover that there is potential for a desirable win-win deal.

> # Brilliant questions should stimulate discovery of understanding in the buyer

Brilliant Questions Promote Sincere Listening for Understanding on the Part of the Seller and They Arouse an Eager Want in the Buyer

When you put aside your own welfare, in favor of understanding your buyer, you demonstrate real intent to help—to work in the best interest of the buyer. Your brilliant questions help you to be a real problem solver. Listening empowers you with understanding.

Even more, your brilliant questions empower both you and your buyer with one more essential element—discovery on the part of your buyer that the she has real needs which you can be entrusted to solve!

I sometimes hear people speak of the skill of a salesperson with comments like, "He's a great salesperson. He could sell curling irons to bald men." While these comments are intended to be high praise, they actually reflect the idea that salespeople are unscrupulous and self-serving.

For that reason, efforts to improve sales skills and sales performance can be misconstrued as tips and techniques to manipulate or bully other people. That is not what the Griffin Hill Sales System is about nor is it what brilliant questions are about.

The purpose of brilliant questions is to put the salesperson in the position of the buyer—to help the seller to see the challenges, difficulties and problems the buyer faces. Brilliant questions help the seller to understand the thoughts and worries of the buyer. They are sincere and empathetic. Any attempt by the salesperson to use brilliant questions to manipulate the buyer in self-serving ways lacks integrity and will ultimately fail. Brilliant questions promote sincere listening on the part of the buyer which fosters understanding and builds a foundation of trust.

Understanding the needs and wants, the thought process and the worries of a buyer will help the salesperson to better serve the interests of that buyer. Armed with the answers to brilliant questions, master salespeople solve problems and provide value for their customers. When sellers demonstrate an ability to make life better and provide a return on investment they arouse in their buyer an eager want for the seller's product or service.

The idea of arousing an eager want in others originated with Harry A. Overstreet who is the former chair of the Department of Philosophy and Psychology at City College of New York.

In his book *Influencing Human Behavior*, Overstreet asserts that all of human action flows from that which we most fundamentally desire. For that reason, he gives this advice to would-be persuaders, "first, arouse in the other person an eager want."[2] Brilliant questions help both buyer and seller to discover that which the buyer most fundamentally desires. A seller with a sincere interest in meeting fundamental needs and wants will enjoy trust and prosperity.

Advance the sale without being deceitful or strictly self-serving

Brilliant Means Effective, Compelling, Productive, Elevating, Discovery-Inciting, Inspired, Genius-Filled, Results-Generating, and Winning

The element of buyer discovery is essential for the salesperson to be empowered to help and entrusted to do so. Helping buyers to arrive at the moment of discovery that they have a need that you can solve is at once elevating and exhilarating. Your questions are brilliant because they help to advance the sale without being deceitful or strictly self-serving. Because your questions are effective at advancing the sale they are productive and help to create a win-win scenario. No wonder they are brilliant!

Brilliant Questions are Purposeful & Advance the Sale

Your questions are not simply a meandering interrogation—aimless and ill prepared. Brilliant questions start with hypotheses about the buyer's needs and wants. The pattern of your questioning tests your hypotheses. Brilliant Questions means there is no one question that does the job. It is the pattern—the sequence of questions that facilitates discovery. The pattern also builds trust as you listen and come to understanding.

Brilliant Questions Help You Navigate Potential Land Mines of Ignorance and Poor Preparation; They Protect You Against Being Patronizing

Poor questions can be land mines—explosive and dangerous. They can expose ignorance or a lack of preparation. Worse yet are the dangerous landmines exposing a lack of understanding and professionalism. Where ignorance and poor preparation just make the salesperson look incompetent, a lack of understanding and professionalism makes you look uninterested, insincere, self-serving and dishonest. While salespeople are taught that questions are useful—important even, they are mostly poorly trained in their use. These salespeople create a sense of "hitting the checklist" required of their sales manager or that they are following some other ill-advised counsel to "question your way to sales success."

Just asking questions is not going to be successful for you. Asking Brilliant Questions is the key. Your questions are only brilliant if they help you to successfully navigate dangerous land mines. If you are perceived as ill-prepared or ignorant; self-serving or dishonest, you will never be able to help the buyer solve their most important problems. You will likely not even discover what they are.

Brilliant Questions are Easily Answered

Questions that are patronizingly obvious or condescending are easily answered. An example of patronizing is, "do you want to increase productivity and profits?" The common theory of these questions is that building a sequence of yes answers will habituate the buyer so that when you ask them to buy they will respond with a yes because they are conditioned to do so. The reality is that this kind of questioning progressively aggravates the buyer rather than facilitating discovery. As you will see from the examples in this book, brilliant questions are easily answered and they advance mutual discovery. Easily answered questions that advance the sale are brilliant!

Brilliant Questions May Be Preceded by Leading Statements

John Ridley Stroop conducted breakthrough research on human cognition, mental priming and interference[3] that is still considered the gold standard for understanding mental processes. The research of Dr. Stroop can help salespeople to be more effective and more persuasive.

At the time Stroop was studying mental processing, psychology was dominated by behaviorists like Pavlov, Watson and Skinner. Simplistically, the behaviorist approach was to introduce a stimulus and elicit a response.

If the desired response was produced, the subject was rewarded if anything other than the desired response was produced the reward was withheld or a punishment was inflicted. Using these methods subjects could be trained or conditioned to deliver the desired behaviors. Behaviorist thinking dominated psychology for decades and overshadowed the work done by Stroop whose research argued for a higher level of sophistication in human cognition and thinking processes. The work of Dr. Stroop demonstrated that what we say and do can influence the mental processes of others. In Stroop's studies, words and actions of researchers influenced the discoveries made by the subjects. In this way thoughts and discoveries influenced conclusions, decisions and behaviors of subjects.

Skillfully selected, our words can facilitate others to think in a targeted direction and pattern. The opposite is also true. The words and questions used by unskilled salespeople can trigger interference with a desired thought process, behavior, conclusion, or decision.

Leading questions prepare the mind; they can prime the cognitive processes of our buyers

What an amazing discovery for salespeople!

The words we use, our manner speech and action can actually facilitate what our buyers think, the conclusions they reach and the way they behave! The power of the Griffin Hill Sales System is that it is based on the science. When you understand the science and apply it, you can increase persuasive power.

The influence of Dr. Stroop and other remarkable scientists is reflected in the Griffin Hill Sales System. The scientific disciplines of human cognition, human performance technology and persuasion research are deeply imbedded in the Griffin Hill Sales System. They are the fabric that make up the patterns and the persuasive power of the system.

As it relates to Brilliant Questions, the science suggests that leading statements can be a powerful tool to influence the thinking of our buyers. Leading questions prepare the mind; they can prime the cognitive processes of our buyers. Leading statements can channel thinking and get things moving in the right direction. Leading statements prime the prospect to understand and value the question. Leading statements help the salesperson and the buyer to stay on track. Leading statements help avoid answers that are tangential to the real issues.

Leading statements can introduce a topic so that the buyer is prepared to think in that direction.

> **Many of our top clients are wrestling with_____. Tell me about ____ as it relates to your organization.**

> **Current industry research suggests ____ as an important consideration. How does ____ figure in to your future planning and decision making?**

> **A recent article in the Wall Street Journal predicted that ____ would be a major issue in the near future. What steps are you taking now with regard to _____?**

Leading statements can also suggest a conclusion that might be reached.

> **Because of the recent pattern of failures with _____, many of our top customers are moving away from ___. What are your plans?**

> **Current research is influencing many in your industry to _____. What is the thinking here at XYZ company?**

> **With the predictions of _____ in recent press coverage many companies are rethinking their future actions. How is current public sentiment guiding your thoughts?**

Brilliant questions can be made even more powerful with appropriate use (not overuse) of leading statements. Sprinkling our discovery activities with leading statements can keep both the seller and buyer focused. Occasional use of leading statements can prepare the buyer's mind for an important topic. Good leading questions can suggest potential conclusions, decisions, and actions. Leading statements can help create Brilliant Questions.

Both Closed-Ended and Open-Ended Questions Can Be Brilliant

Closed ended questions are used to confirm facts and inferred meaning. Closed ended questions can also be used to secure a commitment.

What I heard you say is that your current system is outdated and functionally obsolete. Did I get that right? (confirming facts)

When you tell me your current process produces an unacceptably high error rate, can I safely assume that you intend to change your system? (confirming inferred meaning of facts)

If I can get the agreement back to by noon today, will you make sure it gets to legal before the end of day? (securing commitment)

Open Ended questions stimulate deep cognitive processing, thought and discovery. Using the right type of question to accomplish the desired purpose is brilliant!

You tell me that only 25% of your team is performing to quota. What problems does that create? (pain discovery)

In what way does that create risk or competitive disadvantage for your company in the competitive market? (preservation discovery)

How is low achievement affecting employee morale? (pleasure discovery)

How does your team performing below expectations impact the way you are perceived by upper management?

It seems that missing performance standards would affect profits in two ways: higher costs and lost opportunities. How are your profits impacted by poor performance relative to quota? (profit discovery with lead question)

Drill Down Questions Invite Further Discussion

Using questions to seek more information and greater clarity is what we mean by drilling down. These drill down questions are the heart of conversation that leads to understanding.

They facilitate a deeper dive which can lead to discoveries. Drill down questions help to advance the conversation in a productive and purposeful way. Drill down questions relate to topics already introduced and help you get greater specificity on features and functionality. Drill down questions help you test hypotheses you have made about the prospective buyer and how your product or service might be beneficial to them.

Drill down questions come in three forms: general drill down, Effects Queries, and Consequences Queries. General drill down questions start the process. They seek more information and clarification about statements made by the buyer. Effects Queries start the process of mutual discovery. They help buyers understand the impact of circumstances, situations and decisions. Consequence Queries go even deeper. Consequence queries stimulate discovery of the value proposition. They help make the business case for buying your product or service.

Examples include:

General Drill Down

Tell me more about your buying process.

When is the problem you're describing most likely to occur?

Can you share more about your view on_____?

Effects Queries

What are the effects of____ (recent statement) on ___ your focus.

How is a loss of focus impacting employee productivity? (effects)

What percentage of productivity is being lost? (effects)

How many employees does that affect? (status quo, effects, consequences)

What is the compensation rate of those employees? (status quo, effects, consequences)

So you are saying that 25 employees that you pay $60,000/year are losing 15% in productivity as a result of _____ did I get that right? (summary of facts closed ended question, effects)

Consequences Queries

If my math is right that is costing you $225,000 per year right now. If we can solve just half of that problem you would get a 5x return on your $25,000 investment. What would that do for (value proposition discovery, consequences)?

Profitability? (profit benefit, consequences)

Employee morale? (pain relief, pleasure benefits, consequences)

Exploitation of new market opportunities? (prestige, pleasure, preservation, profit benefit, consequences)

What does that mean for_____?

Combination

> **You tell me you're not getting guidance on safety programs from your current provider.** (leading statement)
>
> **Can you tell me more about that?** (general drill down)
>
> **How is a lack of guidance influencing your creation and implementation of a safety program.** (pain, effects)
>
> **What is the effect of a poor safety program on insurance premiums.** (profit, effects)
>
> **If our safety manager could help you develop better safety programs and lower premiums by 20% or more how would that impact your overall risk budget?** (consequences)

Get all query examples in one handy cheatsheet at **griffinhill.com/brilliant**

Open Ended questions allow the buyer to share. During the Needs Audit stage of the sales process, salespeople should talk only about 20%-40% of the time. The buyer should be doing most of the talking.

25

Even though the buyer is doing most of the talking, the salesperson remains in control of the direction and flow by the pattern and cadence of the questions they use. Open ended questions encourage the buyer to talk and simultaneously help the salesperson to remain in control and on topic.

Open ended questions make the prospect think. They facilitate discovery. Closed ended question are used to get specific information, confirm information and assumptions and secure commitment. Both open ended and closed ended questions are used—each for their appropriate purpose, to facilitate discovery through drill down on effects and consequences.

Brilliant Questions are Majestic

Brilliant questions are majestic. The majesty is born in the underlying science of human cognition. It is developed by following the standards for using open ended and closed ended questions. Majesty is manifest in the discoveries stimulated in salesperson and buyer. It is demonstrated in the persuasive power that stacks the odds of success in favor of getting to a win-win deal by salespeople who are masters of the Brilliant Question.

SECTION II

SYSTEMS

Chapter Four

The System: A Thin Slice of Magic

George Washington Acquired the Magic of Method

Just months before he died, at age 76, Washington Irving completed his five-volume biography of George Washington. Writing of George Washington's boyhood, Irving observed, "…in his earliest days, there was perseverance and completeness in all his undertakings. Nothing was left half done, or done in a hurried and slovenly manner. The habit of mind thus cultivated continued throughout life."[4] If this description speaks highly of George Washington, the man, Irving's summary statement speaks highly of the effect. "He had acquired the magic of method, which of itself works wonders."

If historian or biographer knew nothing else about the life of George Washington except that as a boy, "he had acquired the magic of method," they could rightly predict that the boy's end would be successful and prosperous.

From all our research, one thing stands clear—we are all the product of the systems we employ. Each individual and every organization are subject to systems whether we know it or not. Sometimes our systems are the sum of habits and patterns casually acquired and unconsciously adopted.

31

Sometimes, as in Washington's case, our systems are the result of careful study, thought, analysis, and decision. In either case, our results over time are directly connected to the systems we have developed. Though short term results may be the off-spring of circumstance, George Washington suffered more than one defeat, our long-term results are determined by our over-arching systems, included how we deal with adversity and opposition. The same magic of method displayed in the life of George Washington was evident in the assiduity to true principles displayed by top sales performers in our research.

> ## Our results over time are directly connected to the systems we have developed

Having identified, organized and categorized the elements of effective systems for top sales performers, we found that it was a simple thing to teach the principles and techniques to others. That sales is an art is undisputed. But that it is also a science—a technology even—is a surprising discovery for many people. At Griffin Hill, we soon confirmed that teaching the magic of sales methodology could rapidly change results, in positive ways, for individual salespeople and companies.

A Selling Technology

One definition of a technology is "all the terminology, principles, processes, methods, and techniques related to a given subject, topic, or discipline."

Once the system for selling was reduced to a common terminology and language we found we could begin to teach its principles, processes, methods and techniques to other people with great success.

One team at Xerox shortened their sales cycle from 18 months to under 4 months and a struggling salesperson became a top performer.

A Professional Employer Organization (PEO) whose market position was slipping, replaced their entire sales team, one that was entrenched and unwilling to adapt, with new sellers who were willing to learn and follow the system. Within 90 days new sales revenues were up 408% from the same quarter previous year. In the next 90 days, the sales improvement trajectory continued at nearly 400% over the same quarter in the previous year. The third and fourth quarters showed marked improvement still, with results over 600% and 1000% respectively when compared with same quarters in the previous year.

These early results proved to us, at Griffin Hill, and to our clients that our system could help sales artists to become even more skilled, to perform at ever higher levels and to be able to do so persistently over time.

33

Our Griffin Hill Sales System constituted a new technology for sales and selling. We could teach it and sellers could learn it. It was a marvelous breakthrough in human performance technology relative to sales! Salespeople that embrace the new Griffin Hill technology of sales and selling will experience rapid, substantial and sustainable results!

As a result of our research, we are now able to say with great confidence that there are four essential elements to any system of human performance. Those elements are: process, plays, metrics, and coaching.

There you have it. The magic of method for sales professionals and sales leaders; for entrepreneurs and business people. A discussion of the metrics and coaching aspects of the system would divert our focus from the purpose of this text. However, understanding process and plays is central to that purpose. So let's explore both process and plays.

Be Brilliant!

Chapter Five

Process: A Stepwise Approach to Prosperity and Success

Keep the Process Simple

We learned from the research that process is best kept simple. Some companies had entire booklets describing the steps and flow of their sales process complete with diagrams, arrows and flow charts. IN EVERY CASE, we found these process descriptions to be ineffective at best. At worst, they interfered with the real work productivity of the salespeople. Lengthy processes were universally ignored.

The Magic Number Seven, Plus or Minus Two

The fact that complex processes are eschewed is no surprise to the student of human cognition and performance. The science would predict exactly the behavior that we observed. George A. Miller of the Princeton University Department of Psychology demonstrated that complexity reduces efficacy and adherence simply because it overwhelms working memory!

Dr. Miller's seminal research on working memory was captured in his now famous and often cited paper entitled, "The Magic Number Seven, Plus or Minus Two"[5]. Largely as a result of the work done by Dr. Miller, cognitive science has long acknowledged that the number of objects or elements that can be held in working memory is 5-9 objects. This follows what we have come to know as Miller's Law of seven plus or minus two.

From our research, we knew that process is fundamental. It provides the structure for the rest of the system. Process influences plays, which are the principles and activities that stack the odds of success in favor of the performer. Process influences metrics. It determines what is most important to measure and why. Process also influences training, teaching and coaching—leadership behaviors intended to elevate sales results. Process is like the footings and foundation of a building. Getting process right is fundamental. If the foundation is sound, it positively influences every other aspect of building integrity.

We knew the process had to be simple—9 or fewer steps, closer to 5 is better. It also had to be sophisticated enough to deal with the complexity of interaction among complicated human beings with their own experiences and opinions. The Process had to be robust enough to handle the complexity of a selling experience from beginning to end.

Six Steps to Prosperity

As we tested, observed, innovated and tested again, we ultimately discovered that the simplest way to parse the problem of 'how to get a sale' is a six-step process. Four of the six steps are essential for every selling situation. Two of the steps are optional and are used only when the complexity of the selling situation demands. We chose names for these six steps that are descriptive of their function. Other than that, the names are not sacred and are easily changed to adapt to the culture of any organization.

The six steps of the sales process are:

1. Case Open
2. Needs Audit
3. Solution Presentation
4. Adapted Solution
5. Closing Interaction
6. Fulfillment and Follow-up

The two optional steps are Adapted Solution and Closing Interaction. These steps are used when a sales cycle is either long or complex or both.

The sales process begins with the initial contact and follows the subsequent steps through to completion—either a sale or a "no thanks." This Process defines the milestones along the sales path so that salespeople can clearly see where they are and what steps to take next. The advantages of the Griffin Hill Sales Process include:

Salespeople embrace a common language that brings duplicable results.

A common language engenders a positive and winning sales culture for the organization. This positive culture is fueled by rich communication and a superior ability to identify and share best practices which elevates team performance.

The six steps provide a structure that guides salespeople through each sale.

Advantages & Benefits of a New Technology of Sales

The advantages of the Griffin Hill Sales Process are unique and powerful when compared to any other approach to sales and selling.

When implemented, the benefits are distinct and profitable:

- Salespeople gain a new level of confidence and professionalism that is recognized by suspects and prospects. Confidence is a proven element of persuasive power. It leads to higher close rates and greater financial success.

- Sales cycles are shortened. Unqualified prospects are automatically purged from the pipeline when there is no progress. Additionally, qualified prospects progress more rapidly with a clearly identified and skillfully navigated path.

- With a shorter sales cycle, business volume increases. Salespeople stop wasting time with unqualified prospects. They spend more time with buyers that actually progress toward closing and more buyers move through the pipeline at a faster rate.

- Company image and prestige improves as a new sales culture takes root and the professionalism of your team is recognized in the marketplace.

Steps in the Sales Process

To reiterate, the six steps (or routines) in the Griffin Hill Sales System constitute a clear process. There are six steps in the process:

1. Case Open (CO)
2. Needs Audit (NA)
3. Solution Presentation (SP)
4. Adapted Solution (AS)
5. Closing Interaction (CI)
6. Fulfillment and Follow-up (FF)

The second step in the sales process is the Needs Audit.

It is in the Needs Audit where brilliant questions begin to shine. For that reason, understanding the Needs Audit is fundamental to gaining mastery of brilliant questions. The Needs Audit is the focus of this book.

Chapter Six

Plays: The Play's the Thing

Shakespeare...the Great Sales Guru?

"The play's the things," says Shakespeare's Hamlet, "wherein I'll catch the conscience of the King."[6]

It may not be the king's conscience we aim to catch. But we certainly hope to capture the mind and imagination of our buyer and the play is just the thing to do it! Plays represent important principles from our Griffin Hill research. Our research identified certain principles that super-charge persuasion. They enhance communication and understanding. These plays in their order represent the secret language of persuasion used by top performing salespeople!

One delightful aspect of Plays is that just like in sports or the theater, plays can be tweaked, refined and improved until they have exactly the persuasive effect we are looking for. In this way, Plays become the disciplined expression of principles of success and persuasion. Most certainly, the Play's the thing wherein we capture the imagination, the heart and the hope of the King that is our buyer!

In the Griffin Hill Sales System, Process lays out the general path, but Plays mobilize Process.

Where Process signifies the milestones of the path, Plays define the small steps that lead from one Process milestone to the next. Plays represent principles of human cognition, communication and persuasion—all put into action.

From Building Blocks to Routines

By itself, Process represents the major milestones which are steps of the sales process, Case Open, Needs Audit, Solution Presentation, Adapted Solution, Closing Interactions and Fulfillment and Follow-up. When Process and Plays are combined, together they form a "Routine" in the sales process. It is no longer just a step but it is a complete set of principle-based behaviors that stack the odds of success in our favor.

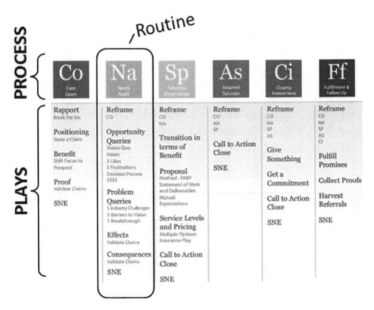

The Power of Principles Expressed as Plays

Because they are principle based, plays can be customized by each salesperson to fit their own style and selling situation adapted to the personality of an individual buyer. In this way, Plays provide a flexible framework where salespeople can apply their own strengths, skills and personality without compromising the integrity of the Process or

Rapid

Substantial

Sustainable

the System. The combination of Process and Plays means each organization and every seller can develop their own customized playbook so they will have a clear plan and path to get to a win-win close. Process and Plays help salespeople to have confidence in every situation and to know what to do next.

Confidence Is Contagious. Your Buyers Catch It From You!

Confidence engendered by process and plays carries over to the way salespeople speak. They speak with greater power and authority. Powerful speech is persuasive speech. According to research scientist Bonnie Erickson and her collaborators, confidence exhibited in the way people speak had a powerful and influential effect[7]. When people were more confident in their speech, they were perceived as more expert, more trustworthy and hence more credible. The combination of confidence, perceived trustworthiness, expertise and credibility elevate persuasive power.

Stack the Odds in Your Favor!

Plays stack the odds of success in favor of the salesperson.

The likelihood of a positive outcome is enhanced when the salesperson has an action plan and is practiced in the art of its execution. As a result, salespeople using the Griffin Hill Sales System close at a higher rate. Salespeople and companies that adopt our sales system experience rapid, substantial and sustainable increases in new sales and revenue.

Brilliant Questions are the Heart of the Needs Audit Routine

Brilliant questions are really just the Plays we use in the Needs Audit Routine. We can dial up any Play (or brilliant question) we need based on the situation. These plays help stack the odds of success in favor of the seller who is skilled in the Griffin Hill Sales System. The Plays of the Needs Audit Routine are structured around four question types: Opportunity Queries, Problem Queries, Effects Queries, and Consequences Queries.

Each question type has a specific purpose—just like a play in athletics, different question types are used to accomplish different objectives. One purpose of this book is to help you understand each question type. Understanding puts your feet firmly on the path of sales mastery!

Chapter Seven

5 Basic Purposes of Brilliant Questions in the Needs Audit

5 Purposes

There are five basic purposes associated with the Needs Audit Routine:

- Get information needed to build a compelling proposal

- Build relationship with buyers

- Stimulate discoveries in decision makers and help them reach conclusions

- Break down emotional barriers and defenses

- Qualify for need, want, ability to pay, and decision making

Get Information Needed to Build a Compelling Proposal

Information and knowledge are power. When salespeople are armed with information and knowledge, they possess the power to influence the buyer. Every professional seller knows the importance of identifying the needs and wants of the buyer that will match the products and services offered by the seller. Securing basic information is the role of Opportunity Queries and Problem Queries in the Needs Audit Routine. Opportunity Queries and Problem Queries are designed to help the salesperson sort out what information is important. They help sellers stay focused on what is really important by understanding the needs and wants of the buyer.

Build Relationships with Buyers

A repeated lesson from our research was that buyers buy benefits—not features. What we also learned is that buyers buy benefits from people they like and trust. It shouldn't be such a surprising discovery, but what we learned was that listening builds liking and trust. Listening and summarizing with reframe plays builds liking and trust even faster. When a salesperson asks a question—the buyer weighs liking and trust in the balance. Greater liking and greater levels of trust elicit more authentic and useful answers—rich with information that can help buyer and seller reach a win-win outcome.

Information given by buyers is wrapped in packets of trust and delivered to the seller. What the seller does with the information helps a buyer determine whether or not the seller is trustworthy. The Plays of the Needs Audit Routine, executed with integrity and honor are essential to liking and trust. The question-answer exchange between buyer and seller is an exercise in relationship building. Get it right and everyone wins. Get it wrong and you lose! Buyers buy benefits. Buyers buy benefits from people they like and trust. Brilliant Questions asked in the right way at the right time and in the right order stimulate liking and trust.

Stimulate Discoveries in Decision Makers and Help Them to Reach Conclusions

Salespeople are generally clear on the need to get information that will help them to build a compelling proposal. What they universally overlook and overwhelmingly neglect, according to our research, is the importance of using questions to stimulate discoveries in decision makers. Stimulating discoveries in decision makers is where the richest veins of gold are found! The philosophy of the Needs Audit is to use Query Plays with a progressive drill-down technique. The drill-down technique starts with Opportunity Query Plays and Problem Query Plays but it is most powerful when used in the Effects Queries and Consequences Queries. These plays form a pattern of brilliant questions that stimulate discoveries in their buyer.

51

It is a progressive discovery process. First, the buyer experiences shadows of dissatisfaction. Next, buyers discover that they need and want the solutions offered by the seller. Discovering a need and want stimulates an intent to act. The next discovery is the epiphany of value. The epiphany of value stimulates the decision to buy.

Break Down Emotional Barriers

We have already mentioned the lack of trust as one of the emotional barriers that gets in the way of a close. Remember the powerful truth from our research—both in the field with more than 3500 professional sellers, and in scientific studies of skilled researchers—that buyers buy benefits from people they like and trust. Humans are a boiling test tube of hormones, chemicals

> # The epiphany of value stimulates the decision to buy

and emotions. Our emotions range widely—fear, angst, pain, desire, want, sad and happy. Some of those emotions get in the way of the buyer/seller relationship. The Needs Audit Routine is an important way to alleviate negative emotions and stimulate those that are positive. The Needs Audit Routine lets the air out of the emotion balloon and alleviates the pressure associated with it.

Qualify for Need, Want, Ability to Pay, and Decision Making

Getting to a win-win deal is the progressive qualification of the buyer. In the Case Open Routine, we qualify for only one thing: interest. In the Needs Audit Routine there are additional qualification hurdles. An important principle we learned from top performing sellers is that qualification isn't just a noun defining the height or the hurdle. It isn't merely a test of already existing qualities where the role of the salesperson is to plumb the nature and characteristics of the buyer to see if they measure up. For top sales performers, qualification is an active process. Further, for top sales performers, the verb *to qualify* didn't simply mean it is an action verb for the buyer. But rather, qualification is an active collaborative process for both buyer and seller. This active collaboration around need, want, ability to pay and decision making process is one of the powerful aspects of the Needs Audit Routine.

Chapter Eight

5 Guiding Principles
of the Needs Audit Routine

5 Principles

Like the 5 basic purposes, there are 5 principles that guide our use of the Plays in the Needs Audit Routine. The principles include: listen, ask Open-ended questions, sharing builds trust, engage in purposeful interactions ("face-time"), and position—persuade but don't sell.

Listen

Recruiters and leaders who evaluate and hire salespeople often mistake the most important attributes. Too often at the top of the list is *gift of gab, outgoing,* and *gregarious.* The attributes that should be at the top of the list are *trustworthiness* and *ability to listen.* The scientific literature is equally compelling about the importance of good listening skills. It turns out that being a SKILLED listener is far more important in persuasion than being gregarious, outgoing or having the gift of gab.

(handwritten margin notes:) HOW CAN I RAISE AND GET THIS... I THINK I AM BAD AT THIS... I HATE THIS WRONG WORDS... WE TAKE THIS

55

For that reason, we have a variety of coaching sessions, trainings and tools designed to elevate understanding of the principles of listening. These coaching sessions help sellers develop listening skill that leads to mastery.

Fundamentally, Boyd Matheson got it right. "if you must speak, ask a question." Learning to effectively run the Query Plays of the Needs Audit Routine will help you to become a better listener. Beware however, you are not asking questions just to check a box or report back to the sales manager that you did it. Don't pre-occupy your mind with what you will ask next or what you will say next. Pay attention to what the buyer is saying. Seek to understand her meaning. As you will see from the Plays, reframing and drilling down are techniques that will help you to become a more skilled listener.

Ask Open-Ended Questions

In the Needs Audit Routine, the buyer should do most of the talking. I frequently use a 20/80 ratio to guide salesperson behavior. During the Needs Audit, sellers talk 20 percent of the time, no more than 40 percent. At this stage of the sales process, talking consists of three essential behaviors: restating, asking questions, and validating buyers. Asking brilliant open-ended questions will stimulate a comfortable flow of talking and sharing on the part of the buyer while avoiding any hint of interrogation.

Sharing Builds Trust

Because buyers buy benefits from people they like and trust, the Needs Audit Routine is designed to build authentic liking and trustworthiness. Again, Plays matter and question order counts when running the Query Plays of the Needs Audit Routine. Asking questions that push for too much too early erodes trust. Following the play-set will guide sellers to the right cadence of questions.

It is not enough to act as though you are worthy of the trust of your buyers. You must actually be a person of character, integrity and honesty. Do what your mom taught you, "behave yourself."

A further study of trust would be a useful endeavor for any sales professional. The world's leading expert on trust is Stephen M. R. Covey. His book entitled *The Speed of Trust* should be in the reference library of every salesperson.

Purposeful Interaction "Face-Time"

Our world is busier—faster paced and more demanding—than ever before. Buyers don't want to waste their time any more than you want to waste yours. You must demonstrate your ability to focus on things that are important to the buyer!

One experience from our field research illustrates the value, to the seller, of focusing on your purpose and advancing the sale.

A salesperson, Albert, was a salesperson selling a high-ticket item with a long sales cycle. Albert had been with the company for 2 years but had yet to close a deal. Because the sales cycle was 18 months, it was not a huge concern for management, but his lack of performance was catching their attention. They liked Albert a lot. He seemed to be hard-working and was meeting their minimum standard of being in 25 sales meetings each month. I agreed to work with Albert for the day. We started our planning and I asked about the purpose of our first sales call of the morning. Albert replied simply, "face time." Seeking more understanding, I soon discovered Albert's performance problem. He was being measured by the number of meetings he had each month—not the number of times he advanced a sale. "Face time" was his only objective. Don't fall into the Albert trap. The purpose of a sales call is to advance the sale! The Needs Audit Routine will help you to achieve that objective. Albert became a master of the Griffin Hill Sales System and a top sales performer!

Position: Persuade—Don't Sell

The Query Plays of the Needs Audit Routine will position you to win the business. You will out-maneuver competitors and put yourself in a position to close. The "positioning" part of this principle makes perfect sense. It is the Persuade—Don't Sell part that seems to stand in conflict.

From our field research we discovered that persuasion really occurs when salespeople listen. Salespeople and sales managers often think, in error, that persuasion occurs when the salesperson talks. In correction of this mistaken notion, an important guiding principle of the Needs Audit is to use a pattern of listening—reframing, asking questions and drilling down, that stimulates discovery on the part of the decision maker! When your questions cause buyers to discover that they need and want your product or service they have already reached a decision. You help buyers reach that decision when you ask Effects and Consequences Queries. So you will persuade in the Needs Audit by keeping the focus on the buyer—letting them talk about their goals and their priorities, their needs and their wants.

Chapter Nine

Basic Plays of the Needs Audit Routine

Basic Plays

The Basic Plays of the Needs Audit Routine are:

- Reframe

- Opportunity Queries, Problem Queries, Effects Queries, Consequence Queries (OPEC)

- Schedule the Next Event (SNE)/Permission

In the following chapters, you will learn about the various plays for each type of question. Frequent reframe and constant drill down are essential techniques for running these plays. For that reason, I like to think of the Needs Audit Routine as drilling for oil. It is the cartel of oil producers, Organization of the Petroleum Exporting Countries (an OPEC different from our Opportunities, Problems, Effects and Consequences) that knows all about drilling.

So you can think of the Needs Audit Playset as Reframe, OPEC with drill down, and SNE.

1. Reframe
2. OPEC with Drill Down
3. SNE

Thinking about this Playset as Reframe, OPEC—with drill down, and SNE makes it easy to remember. The OPEC (Opportunity, Problem, Effects and Consequences) queries, help identify areas of interest and begin the process of digging below the surface to gain clarity. Drilling down facilitates discoveries for both the buyer and the seller. The pattern of asking additional clarifying questions is what we mean by "drilling down." Once an area of interest has been identified, we dig beneath the surface to stimulate discovery. Drilling down is simply asking open-ended questions that provide additional information. These Drill Down questions set up powerful effects and consequences queries. Drill Downs can be as simple as:

"Tell me more about that."

"Help me to understand_____."

"Can you explain____ in more detail?"

Drill Down Worker Bees

Rudyard Kipling's serving men are good drill-down worker bees. Questions beginning with who, what, where, when, why and how can add valuable information, clarity and insight.

I keep six honest serving men,
They taught me all I knew,
Their names are What and Why and When
And How and Where and Who.

SECTION III

A GLIMPSE AT THE SCIENCE

Chapter Ten

Introduction to Psychological Factors in Brilliant Questions

Psychology? Honestly!

Like most research scientists, I am skeptical about results of public opinion surveys that I frequently hear reported on the radio or in other news outlets. Some of my skepticism is related to statistical standards like survey size, representative sampling and method of gathering. Even when statistical standards are met, there are questions related to psychological influences that can greatly sway opinion and answers to survey questions. The words used to ask questions, response options and question order are all psychological factors related to the validity of survey results and their interpretation.

These psychological factors are important in sales. Skilled and well-intentioned salespeople can shoot themselves in the foot just by the words they use, by the order in which they ask questions or the options offered. Once an opinion is given—no matter what psychological factors influenced its creation—it is astonishingly difficult to dissuade the responder from the hastily and erroneously formed opinion.

This psychological phenomenon goes by many names. For me, the most descriptive is *belief perseverance*.

Belief Perseverance

One highly regarded study of belief perseverance was conducted by Anderson, Lepper and Ross[8]. The researchers created fictitious characters, fire fighters, for whom work files were created. Frank was described as a cautious, safety first kind of guy. He had a stellar and decorated career as a firefighter. The other file described George. He too was cautious and safety-minded. But unlike Frank, George's file described him as a problem employee with a troubled history and a checkered record. The respective files were studied by the research subjects. One group read Frank's file; the other read George's. The group was then asked to offer opinions on what factors make for either a great fire fighter or one that was not likely to shine.

Predictably, those reading Frank's file thought caution and safety made for a good fire fighter. Those reading George's file thought caution was the mark of someone destined to fail in this line of work. No surprises so far right? The surprise comes in what happened next. Subjects were informed that the files were fictitious and that those reading the other file—the one they had not read, reached the exact opposite conclusion.

The manipulation now unmasked, subjects in each group were queried about their opinions regarding attributes of individuals likely to succeed or fail as firefighters. Despite unmasking the subterfuge, the opposing opinions remained largely unchanged!

The 1-2 Punch of Field Research and Scientific Literature

Psychological factors are crucial to the way people form and hold onto opinions. For that reason, in addition to the field research that studied more than 3,500 salespeople and nearly half a million sales interactions, our study of the scientific literature guided the shaping of the Griffin Hill Sales System. The scientific literature informed our understanding of what we observed in the field. It clarified salesperson behavior and buyer response. The 1-2 punch of field research and scientific literature review shaped what we believe to be the most powerful system available for sales and selling.

When it comes to understanding the science of persuasion in sales and selling, we have a large lead over the rest of the pack and we don't intend to relinquish that lead. For that reason, we continue to advance practical research among sellers and buyers. We also continue to monitor the scientific literature as well as conduct our own studies into the psychology of sales and selling.

Though a comprehensive view is impossible in this book, it is useful to have at least a glimpse at some of the scientific research.

Chapter Eleven

Spreading Activation: Frame Of Mind

Did I Really Just Read That?

You may have experienced the same psychological phenomenon as I have. On more than one occasion, while reading a book, I find that I have turned more than a few pages, my eyes passing over every word, and yet I have no conscious awareness about what happened in the storyline. My thoughts have wandered and they are seemingly unconnected to what I am reading. Somehow, in my mind, I got to a white sand beach with beautiful sapphire waters spreading out before me. I have no awareness of how my mind wandered to that remote paradise or what triggered the departure from my book. For me, this is an example of the cognitive process of spreading activation theorized by Collins and Quillian and many subsequent cognitive scientists.

Is It Board or Bored?

Collins and Quillian used spreading activation as a theoretical model to understand semantic memory and how it functions[9].

The idea is that we have a set of words and their respective definitions stored in our memory. They lie dormant in our memory until activated by some stimulus, like the book we are reading or the conversation in which we are engaged. When we hear a word thus stored, that item is activated in our memory along with a simple definition. For example, we hear "board." The word is activated along with its definition, "a piece of wood." An interesting aspect theorized by cognitive scientists, is that once "board" is stimulated or activated it has the effect of spreading to or stimulating other words with related meaning. In other words, once "board" is activated in our semantic memory, activation will spread to words like "2x4", "wood", "construction", "plank"—perhaps even "bored", a word related in sound but not in definition.

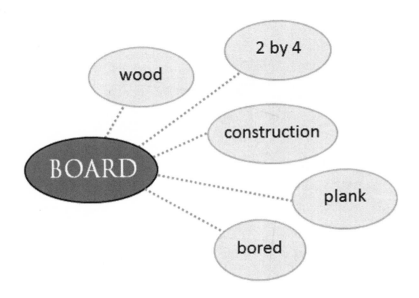

I like to think of spreading activation as a set of pixels in the brain that behave like tuning forks. When one pixel is stimulated or "activated", its activation resonates with related pixels and they, in turn, are activated and light up. All the related meaning is now alive and available in our active memory—no longer dormant, and it acts to provide richness and meaning to our current conversation.

With successive activation, however, the connection to the original trigger or stimulus can be lost. We are not exactly sure how we got from the storyline of our murder mystery to the sunny Caribbean beach that exists only in our mind.

Here is a simple example from a little experiment with a small group of people. I informed the group that I would give them a stimulus word and asked that they write the first word that came to their mind. The trigger word was "fire hydrant." Fire hydrant was the first word to "light up" in the semantic memory of my spontaneous research project. Once fire hydrant lit-up, it resonated in a way that stimulated other words to also "light up."

The results were:

- Two people said *water*

- One reported *red*

- One said *fire*

- 5 people said *dog*

Maybe these are some of the same pixels that "lit up" in your mind. It is very easy to see the connection between fire hydrant and water, red, fire and dog.

We took the experiment one more step. Again, I promised a one word stimulus to which they were to write the first word that came into their mind. I used as the trigger word, "water", one of the response words from the first round.

The answers were:

- 3 said *drink*

- 2 said *thirsty*

- 1 each said fountain, ocean, wet, boat

Again, the connection between the trigger word "water" and the related words "thirsty," "fountain," "drink," "ocean," "wet," and "boat," is easily understood. It is also easy to see that the trigger word "fire hydrant" produced a connection to "water" and that "water" as a trigger word produced "boat." However, if we eliminate the connecting word, "water," it is not easy to see how we got from "fire hydrant" to "boat." In this way, a series of connecting words can lead from the storyline of our murder mystery to the beach in paradise, leaving us unsure as to how we got there.

Cognition and Sales...Distant Cousins?

So, how does this cognitive science relate to sales? The words you use and the questions you ask trigger or activate concepts and ideas in the mind of your buyer. If your questions are random, you produce random thinking on the part of your buyer. If, however, your questions are patterned, they can stimulate a discovery in your buyer that they need and want your product or service. The drill-down technique of the Needs Audit can guide the thoughts of your buyer through the chain of logic that results in their self-discovery.

Understanding and using the principle of spreading activation in the sales process is not mind-control nor is it slimy manipulation. You cannot use this principal to back people into a mental corner that they don't want to be in. There are other cognitive processes that protect us from that kind of mental manipulation, including cognitive dissonance—the unsettled feeling that something just isn't right. We might not be able to put our finger on what is causing the unsettled feeling, but we will know it and it protects us from mental bullying.

Sincere or Slimy?

It is valuable to remember that we use what we learn about human cognition with a sincere intent to help and serve prospective buyers. Using what we learn about human cognition, in that way, is neither dishonest nor is it slimy.

The truth is we are pushing those psychological buttons whether we intend to or not.

Spreading activation occurs in the mind of your buyer whether you know it or not. A great Japanese teacher and mentor, Watanabe Kan San, once taught me this important truth—"you cannot not to teach." No matter what we say or do, for good or ill, we teach observers something about our nature, character, abilities and attributes. Because people are active information processors, our words and behaviors are observed, considered and

You cannot *not* to teach

evaluated. Judgements are made and decisions are reached. "You cannot not to teach." The question is, are you using words and actions to stimulate focused and reasoned thinking in your buyer? The alternative is that you stimulate meandering, confused thought that is not helpful to you or to your buyer.

Being Socrates

Understanding spreading activation helps us to grasp the power of the Socratic Method. The Socratic Method is a form of cooperative dialogue based on asking and answering questions to stimulate critical thinking. The end goal of the Socratic Method is to draw out ideas and to stimulate mutual discoveries.

Understanding spreading activation motivates skillful use of the Socratic Method that both buyers and sellers will find satisfying, helpful, and stimulating as opposed to the clumsy interrogation technique used by the sales novice. Clumsy interrogation techniques result in confusion, frustration, and resistance.

Chapter Twelve

Words Matter: A Glance at the Scientific Literature

Words Matter

The case for mental priming is further advanced by Loftus and Palmer, who showed short clips of automobile accidents to study subjects and asked them to estimate vehicle speed[10]. One group was asked to estimate how fast the cars were going when they bumped into each other. Other groups were asked the same question, replacing the word "bumped" with words like "hit" or "smashed." As you can imagine, estimates of speed were higher when the word "smashed" was used as compared to when "bumped" was used.

Using dense nouns, verbs, adjectives and adverbs enhance the seller's power to stimulate targeted discoveries in their buyers. "Terminating," "extinguishing," or "exterminating pain" is better than "improving conditions." Dense words are explicit and vivid. They stimulate, in the imagination, a vision for a more desirable state.

The power of plays is you can think and create, in advance, the dense words that will stimulate discoveries of need and eager want in your buyer. Plays stack the odds of success in favor of skilled sellers with a win-win disposition.

Question Order Counts

Careful attention to detail went into creating the process and plays that make up the Griffin Hill Sales System. In the creation of a system, careful thought was given to the order of the steps in the process and sequencing of plays for each routine. Order and sequence are designed for smooth mental progression. The importance of sequence is illustrated in the research of Schuman and Ludwig (1983). Asked whether "the Japanese government should be allowed to set limits on how much American industry can sell in Japan," most Americans said no. However, in a separate survey more than 60% of American respondents answered yes to the same question! The difference was that respondents in the second survey were first asked whether "the American government should be allowed to set limits on how much Japanese industry can sell in the United States." It turns out that question order influences question answers. Question order also influences the formulation of opinions, decisions and behaviors.

Confident Delivery and Powerful Speech

The perception of credibility and expertise influences persuasive power. In research conducted by Bonnie Erickson and her associates (1978), speaking in a straightforward and confident manner influences the perception of others that the speaker was a credible expert. Credibility and expertise are both factors in persuasive power.

With a system of process and plays, the salesperson is armed with preparation and rehearsal. Preparation helps sellers to act more confidently and to be more confident. Confidence is contagious—buyers catch it from the salesperson. A more confident salesperson is a more persuasive salesperson.

The Power of Simple Systems: George A. Miller

As discussed earlier, the field research and the scientific literature demonstrated the importance of simplicity. Lengthy or complex processes were ignored or adhered to in only a cursory way to appease sales leaders. George A. Miller's paper, "The Magic Number Seven, Plus or Minus Two" (1956), continues to be the gold standard regarding the capacity of working memory and the standard that influenced the creation of The Griffin Hill Sales System. With a process of six simple steps—two of which are optional, we preserve and engage full mental power!

On top of that, there are only 5-6 types of Plays in each sales routine which makes the entire system simple to learn and simple to use. Simplicity helps stack the odds of success in favor of the salesperson!

Summary: Building on a Firm Foundation

More than a decade of hard work and research influenced the creation of the Griffin Hill Sales System. Field research including more than 3,500 salespeople, 144,000 sales cases and nearly half a million sales interactions helped us to discern and catalogue the skills of the top 1% of sales performers.

An intense study of the scientific literature informed our understanding of the data gathered in field research. This tiny glimpse of the scientific principles demonstrates that mental processes are real and they are subject to priming influences. Sales professionals who understand these psychological principles and apply them have greater success.

SECTION IV

PRACTICAL
APPLICATION

Chapter Thirteen

The Plays: Recapturing the Magic of Framing

Time Changes the Frame of Mind

Your positive interaction with a buyer, including plays designed to stack the odds of success in favor of achieving a win-win deal, create a positive frame of mine. The good feeling and positive mood of the buyer is at its peak at the close of your meeting, no matter what stage of the sales process you're in. Step-by-step, every play is carefully designed to create a positive disposition and frame of mind. Each play builds on the positive ground gained by the previous play. Because each step adds to the positive state, the good feelings reach their peak as you wrap-up your sales call. That is very good news! The Plays are doing their job for you.

Now for the not-so-good news. Decay of that positive frame of mind begins immediately when you leave. Your buyer goes on to the next item on her agenda, the next meeting on her calendar, the next problem demanding her attention. She stops thinking about you. She continues to "not think about you" until the date and time of your next appointment.

In the intervening time, the good feeling and intention you built in the previous meeting has slipped away. Your buyer has been pre-occupied with work and life and that changes her frame of mind relative to you, the seller, your company and the products or services you offer. Hence the need to recapture that good will. You need to "reframe," or to reset the frame of mind in your buyer.

> **To reframe means to reclaim the positive mental state you created in the previous meeting**

Reframing

To reframe means to reclaim the positive mental state, attitude, and predisposition you created in the previous meeting. You reclaim that positive mental state in your buyer with a brief summary of the previous meeting by highlighting the basic plays from the previous stage of the sales process.

Because we are in the Needs Audit Routine, the previous stage is the Case Open. The basic plays of the Case Open Routine are Rapport, Position, Benefit, Proof and SNE. The plays of the Case Open Routine worked to create a positive frame of mind in your buyer.

Consider the following examples.

(Rapport Play) Ms. Thomas, it's Scott Baird at Griffin Hill. Our mutual friend, Maria Lopez, suggested I give you a call.

The Rapport Play makes a connection, tells Ms. Thomas who you are and invokes the good feelings Ms. Thomas has about her friend Maria Lopez. That begins the process of stimulating a positive frame of mind

Ms. Thomas: Oh, I haven't seen Maria in several weeks! How is she doing?

Seller: She is doing great. The twins are growing. She says to say, "hi."

Ms. Thomas: That's great. She is such a good person.

Seller: She is a great person and the reason she suggested that I call is her experience with my firm.

(Positioning Play) Griffin Hill is a human and organizational performance company.

(Benefit Play) We help salespeople get more opportunities, more closes and more revenue.

(Proof Play) At Maria's company we boosted revenue by 68% in the first 90 days! Maria thought that would interest you.

The positioning play tells Ms. Thomas what I do. The Benefit Play describes why she should care about what I do and stimulates interest. Who doesn't want more revenue?! The Proof Play quantifies the benefit with verifiable evidence—she can call her friend Maria and confirm that what I say is true. This satisfies her natural skepticism and makes it safe to take a next step.

Ms. Thomas: Well of course increasing revenue interests me. How do I get that same result?

Seller: Whether we can deliver the same result for you is yet to be determined but, ...

(Schedule the Next Event Play (SNE)) I would love to get together and talk about your goals and priorities at XYZ company. Is there a day of the week that is best for you?

The Schedule the Next Event Play (SNE) establishes the purpose of the call—to talk about Ms. Thomas, her goals and her priorities. No risk of a high-pressure sales call here. It is safe to take this meeting. The Case Open Routine creates the right frame of mind.

In the example, it starts with the good feelings associated with Ms. Thomas' friend, Maria and progresses to the reason for my call based on what I do. Without the positioning play, your buyer is confused about the purpose of your call. By using the Positioning Play you alleviate the mind of your buyer. His mind is no longer occupied by that question. Sharing the benefit stimulates curiosity and interest. The Proof Play eases the buyer's skepticism. The Schedule the Next Event Play (SNE) is a natural call to action, a reasonable next step.

By declaring the purpose of the next meeting, which is to talk about Ms. Thomas' goals and priorities, it eliminates the possibility of pressure to buy. The Case Open Routine creates a friendly, positive, curious and safe frame of mind. It is just 5 basic plays. Each play is 12 words or less. The plays are mobilized by concise conversation, just enough to make it flow. The positive disposition is memorialized by getting a specific time and date on the calendar.

Back to the problem. After our call, Ms. Thomas met with an underperforming employee. It didn't go well. She worked on her taxes with the accountant, gave a report to the board and worked with HR to replace the employee she let go. Ms. Thomas has been busy. Her mind has been occupied by the regular course of business. Several days pass and Ms. Thomas is sitting in her office and the secretary comes in and announces, "Ms. Thomas, Scott Baird is here for your 2:00 PM appointment."

Ms. Thomas (thinking Scott Baird? Who is Scott Baird? And why do I have a 2:00 PM appointment with him? How did he get on my calendar?) says, "Yeah, okay. Show him in."

Seller enters: "Ms. Thomas, so great to meet you. I'm Scott Baird. You'll remember that our mutual friend Maria is responsible for getting us together."

Ms. Thomas (thinking, Oh yeah, the sales guy. Great, I really don't have time for this.) says pleasantly and with a smile, "Yes, of course. How are you today?"

The fact that we are meeting at all is a credit to the SNE Play doing its job. We memorialized the positive frame of mind with a commitment for an appointment that has a specific time, date and place and with a mutually-understood purpose. And now re-invoking the name of our mutual friend Maria earns enough good will to keep the appointment and the courtesy of a pleasant smile.

Here's how the rest of the Reframe goes:

Seller: I'm terrific thank you. Ms. Thomas, in our previous conversation I shared with you a little bit of what we do as a human and organizational performance company. We help our clients get more revenue just like we did for Maria's company where we increased new sales by 68% in the first 90 days.

We agreed to get together today to talk about what you're doing—your goals and priorities. I've got some questions that will help me understand your current situation. Maybe we could start by you sharing a little bit about the company and what is going on with sales.

The mention of the Position, Benefit and Proof Plays re-kindle interest and reminds Ms. Thomas why she wanted to meet in the first place. The salesperson is able to successfully capture attention and positive attitude, and put Ms. Thomas at ease as we focus attention on her situation and not on a high-pressure selling situation.

Frame of mind includes thoughts, opinions, moods and attitudes. It is the mental state and pre-disposition a buyer has toward a seller and the seller's products and services. The words we use and the questions we ask—including the order in which we ask them, have a powerful effect on what the buyer thinks, the way they drink in, process and decide about information. Plays are tools that wield a powerful influence. Plays have the power to create a positive frame of mind. The passage of time erodes the mental position established by plays. However, the same plays that created the positive frame of mind in the first place can re-establish it.

Plays stack the odds of in favor of the salesperson being able to establish a positive mental state and advance the sales process.

One powerful play that can be used at the beginning of each routine in the sales process is the Reframe Play, a simple summary of the past meeting using the Plays used in that meeting. For good or ill, Plays influence what people think, the conclusions they reach and the way they behave! Best to use Plays that help our cause.

Chapter Fourteen

The Plays: Opportunity Queries

Guided Discovery and Opportunity

In the Needs Audit Routine, we qualify buyers for four things: need, want, decision making, and financial ability to pay. Opportunity Queries help sellers to qualify buyers.

> **Opportunity Queries help you map the terrain and locate the treasure—the opportunity to serve the buyer**

The Needs Audit is a guided discovery activity. A prepared seller guides the discussion and the discovery. Opportunity Queries stimulate discovery for both salesperson and prospect. They help the salesperson identify opportunities for a business relationship. Just like an old west prospector's treasure map where X marked the location of the most productive veins of ore, Opportunity Queries help salespeople to map the terrain and locate the treasure—the opportunity to serve the buyer.

Opportunity Queries can focus the salesperson on the buyer's top goals and priorities. The intersection of the buyer's goals and priorities with the salesperson's products and services creates the perfect X that marks the spot—the opportunity for treasure. That's where the salesperson should focus attention and drill down using effects and consequences queries.

Six Types of Opportunity Queries

There are six types of Opportunity Queries. Each type has an essential role in creating or defining the opportunity. Or in the alternative, disqualifying the prospect because of the lack of opportunity. I like to think about Opportunity Queries in three pairs. Each pair helps identify gaps between desired and actual results.

The six types of Opportunity Queries are:

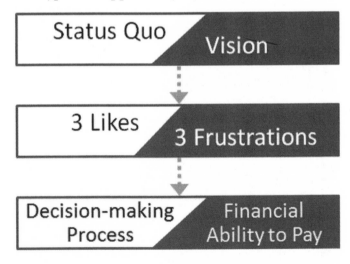

Defining Opportunity

The first pair is Status Quo and Vision. Status Quo Queries identify the current situation and the current results. Vision Queries define the desired state and desired results. Because we all expect to progress, we expect future results to be better than current results. The difference between current results and desired results shines a bright light on the performance or results gap. Where there is a gap, there is an opportunity.

The Second pair is "Three Likes" and "Three Frustrations." This pair gives you a great opportunity to drill down—to get deeper than the surface. The Three Likes Queries and Three Frustrations Queries stimulate clarity of thought in buyers. The clarity of things that are going well in contrast with the clarity of current frustrations creates a satisfaction gap. Dissatisfaction motivates buyers to seek resolution and that creates opportunity.

The final pair is "Decision Making Process" and "Financial Ability to Pay." This pair isn't intended to create gaps in the same way as the other pairs. They are paired because they are essential qualifications that define whether there is an opportunity to do business or not. These two queries are among the most crucial of conversations. The decision-making process must define a clear path to "yes" or there is no opportunity. Even if we get a "yes" but there is no financial ability to pay—there is no opportunity.

Too often, salespeople avoid the crucial conversations around decision making and financial ability to pay. That is a big mistake because they waste time in meetings where there is no opportunity.

Question Order and the Emotional Energy Charge

Remember that question order counts. Notice the order of the Opportunity Query Plays in the context of the emotional energy charge associated with each play type. Creating the right frame of mind means creating the right emotional energy state.

Status Quo Queries have a neutral charge. They are neither positive nor negative. Status Quo Queries are the simple facts. Using Status Quo Queries first allows us to start on neutral emotional ground—safe ground. Too much positive emotion from the salesperson can be off-putting to the buyer. Jumping in with the negative, "what keeps you up at night," can stimulate protective resistance that causes the buyer to shut down rather than open up. Starting with a neutral emotional charge establishes the connection without risk.

Vision Queries carry a positive emotional charge. The desired future state is filled with hope and optimism. There is an enthusiasm about plans to get to a whole new level of achievement. Having first established a connection on neutral emotional ground, we are ready to add positive energy to the sales call.

Adding positive emotional energy into the sales call has the effect of making deposits into the emotional bank account. In his book *The Seven Habits of Highly Successful People*, Stephen R. Covey reminds us that if we don't have a positive balance in the emotional bank account it will be impossible to make a withdrawal. Vision Queries are charged with positive emotional energy that we can draw upon later.

Three Likes also has a positive charge. Having people talk about what they like is positive and enjoyable. Using the Three Likes Play adds to our deposits in the emotional bank account.

Three Frustrations has a negative charge. It is a negative charge in the sense that talking about frustrations can evoke negative emotions including guilt, shame, and embarrassment. By definition, our buyer is frustrated by these conditions or situations and frustration carries a negative emotional charge. However, frustrations are often where the opportunity to make a sale reside and so salespeople often want to jump right in and initiate their inquiry with frustrations, without having first laid the emotional groundwork. Proper question order helps you accumulate positive deposits in the emotional bank account before making this small withdrawal.

Decision Making Process is neutral. Asking about the decision making process after frustrations allows the emotions to return to a state of equilibrium.

Financial Ability to Pay can be sensitive. Sensitivity can put additional demands on our emotional bank account. The good news is we have already made deposits.

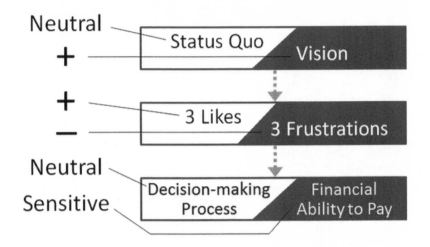

Question order when asking Opportunity Queries helps you to make an emotional connection and make deposits in the emotional bank account. Deposits entitle you to make appropriate withdrawals. The whole process builds trust and strengthens your relationship with buyers.

Chapter Fifteen:

Exploring Each Type of Opportunity Query

Status Quo

The Reframe Play establishes the context for Status Quo and other Opportunity Queries. The discussion and examples that follow are intentionally general. In application, a seller will use the Reframe Play and specific words that channel thoughts and discussion.

The answers sought by some Status Quo Queries are often available from public sources including websites, news releases and published stories. When public sources provide information, it may be useful for the seller to summarize salient points, followed by:

"Did I get that right?"

"Were the articles I studied anywhere near correct?"

"Are the sources I consulted current? Did they get it right?"

Remember that the purpose for using closed-ended questions include confirming information.

The foregoing examples represent the appropriate use for closed-ended questions.

Even though some general information is available from public sources, other basic information is related to the person with whom you are meeting.

"Mr. Olsen, I've been looking forward to meeting. Maybe we could start with you sharing the kinds of things you are doing here at ABC Company."

"That role seems central to our discussion today. Can you tell me more about the tasks and responsibilities related to your role?"

"Can you give me a better feel for the scope and scale?"

"How many production employees are you responsible for?"

Status Quo Queries give the seller a baseline understanding of what is important to the buyer. Here are some examples of general Status Quo Queries:

"What does turnover look like?"

"What is the onboarding process for new employees?"

"Tell me about the training and development process?"

"What does the position include?"

"What are the goals that guide those that you lead"

"What is most important to you?"

"How are they evaluated?"

"How closely are your team members performing to their potential?"

"What do you measure?"

"How do you measure it?"

"Why do you measure it (and why in that way)?"

"How do you (and they) know when they're getting it right?"

"What is your error rate?"

"What are you doing to reduce defect rate?"

"How long have you had your present equipment?"

Some Status Quo Queries can be a little more provocative. They are good clarifying or drill-down questions.

"To what extent have you implemented ____?" (process, solution, training, equipment use)

"How secure are your current contracts and customers?"

"Are you growing or shrinking?"

"What categories are best sellers in that department?"

"Where do you think the market is going."

Often our scenarios assume the interaction between buyer and seller is initiated by the seller. Some Status Quo Queries are used when the buyer is actively shopping—actively seeking a solution, when the buyer initiates the interaction.

"What would you like (the product) to do for you?"

"Who will be the person in charge of the program?"

"When would be the best time to get started?"

"What kind of Corporate Wellness goals are you currently pursuing?

"What kind of program do you prefer?"

Some Status Quo Queries help you identify what kind of a buyer you have. You want to know if your buyer is an economic buyer with profit/loss responsibility.

Is he in a technical role—evaluating features and functionality and other technical aspects? Is he a user of the product or service—looking for ease of use and user interface? Features and functionality are much more important to users and technical buyers. Users are responsive to pain-relief and pleasure benefits. Technical buyers are sensitive to preservation and prestige benefits. Financial benefits are more important for buyers with profit/loss responsibilities.

"What are the specifications for your current equipment?"

"Can you describe the way ____ (the equipment, the process) is being used today?"

"How does your business compare with your projections from a year ago?"

"How is business performance compared to a year ago?"

"What factors do you feel will help your company remain successful?"

These examples should help stimulate ideas for creating Status Quo Queries in your selling situation. Choose Status Quo Queries carefully.

Using too many Status Quo Queries can make a buyer feel like they are being interrogated. Be judicious. Use your Status Quo Queries to stimulate conversation about important topics.

Vision—Best of All Possible Worlds

Vision questions address the goals, hopes, dreams and desires of the buyer. Future hopes always outstrip current performance. The difference between current results and desires for future performance creates a satisfaction gap.

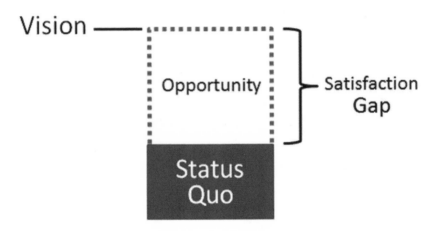

Vision Queries can begin the drill down process.

Seller (SQ): "What is your current rate of growth?"

Buyer: "It's not bad. We're up about 2% over last year."

Seller (VISION) "What is your vision for growth in the upcoming year?"

Buyer: "Ideally, we would like to be closer to 5% maybe even 6% growth."

Seller (SQ): "How does your business compare with your projections from a year ago?"

Buyer: "We're up from last year but we're running behind projections."

Seller (Vision): "In the best of all worlds, how would that look a year from now?"

Buyer: "Well, we certainly want to meet projected revenues and growth. Even more would be better."

Seller (SQ): "How closely are your team members performing to their potential?"

Buyer: "They work hard but it seems like everything is just too casual, not enough urgency."

Seller (Vision): "What would you like that to be next year at this time?"

Buyer: I'd love it if everyone had their head in the game and they focused on the work with more intensity.

Seller (SQ): "How is business performance compared to a year ago?"

Buyer: "We're about the same."

Seller (Vision): "What is your vision for next year?"

Buyer: "We expect better growth, more efficiency and more profits."

Seller (SQ): "What is your error rate?"

Buyer: "We're running too high, probably around 6 errors per 1000 units."

Seller (Vision): "In your ideal world, what would the error rate be?"

Buyer: "We think it should be under 3 per 1,000 and we'd like to get under 2 per 1,000."

Seller (SQ): "What does turnover look like?"

Buyer: "It runs about 10% annually."

Seller (VISION): "With a better _____ (benefits, training, compensation, etc) program, what do you see turnover looking like in the future?"

Buyer: "It should be under 5%. 3% would be great."

Seller (SQ): "What is the onboarding process for new employees?"

Buyer: "It's pretty simple. We give them a desk and a computer. They meet with HR to get a company handbook. That's about it."

Seller (Vision): "What would onboarding look like in your new and improved world?"

Buyer: "We want every employee to have position training and be clear about the expectations for job performance. Everyone needs to know how they will be evaluated and what a home run would look like."

Seller (SQ): "What is the training and development process?"

Buyer: "We do some kind of a corporate meeting once a year."

Seller (Vision): "In the best of all worlds, what elements would be better next year?"

Buyer: "Getting specific job training is a must. Maintaining and advancing skill with ongoing training is a must if we are going to keep up."

Seller (SQ): "Are you growing or shrinking?"

Buyer: "We're staying about the same."

Seller (Vision): "What do you hope for in the 1-3 year horizon?"

Buyer: "It seems that staying about even is really falling behind. We have got to kick it in gear. We want 5-7% growth in the coming year."

Seller (SQ): "What is most important to you?"

Buyer: "Hands down, revenue."

Seller (Vision): "What is your goal for revenue?"

Buyer: *"We want everyone to understand that revenue is job one. We want our revenue generating engine to perform with more horsepower."*

Seller (SQ) "How are employees evaluated?"

Buyer: *"We want them to work hard and have a good attitude."*

Seller (Vision): "What is your vision for improved performance with improved evaluation?"

Buyer: *"We believe that when everyone understands the expectations better, they'll know what they can do to improve productivity."*

Seller (SQ): "What is your current business volume (revenue)?"

Buyer: *"We're at 100,000 units a month."*

Seller (Vision): "In the best of all worlds, where would your production be next year at this same time?"

Buyer: *"We'd love to be doing 150,000 units."*

3 Likes Query

Asking the buyer to share three things they like about the current situation is a positive and encouraging question. It encourages the buyer to celebrate current successes. It helps the seller to know what is important to the buyer. As a seller, your solution should solve an existing problem, but your solution must preserve, enhance or expand the things that are going well. The 3 Likes Query adds positive energy into the conversation and contributes to the emotional bank account. It is a great way to initiate or further drill down on buyer's answers. It also has persuasive power as a standalone question.

Positive drill down on status quo—buyer reports positive results in answer to a Status Quo or Vision Query.

Seller: "it sounds like this is very important to you." What three things do you like best about ____.

Seller: "What three things do you like best about your steady growth."

Seller: "Tell me more about why this is so important (to you, to the company). What three things do you like best about that?"

3 Frustrations Query

Your deposits in the emotional bank account have earned you the right to make a withdrawal. You don't want to overdraw your account but with the right question order, the 3 Frustrations Query is safe. You can use it as a drill down question, or as a separate standalone question. The 3 Frustrations Question works great with a leading statement that primes the mental processes of your buyer.

> **Seller: "Most of our clients have an error rate substantially below what you report. What 3 frustrations do you have about your high error rate."**

> **Seller: "We've talked about a lot of positive things. Let's shift gears just a little bit. What are your 3 biggest frustrations with_____?"**

> **Seller: "Some of our larger customers indicate that model prevented them from handling peak volume. What frustrations have you experienced?"**

Decision Making Process

Asking about the process for making decisions is a crucial conversation. It can't be neglected. As simple as this question is, it's easy to make a mistake. The most frequent error committed by salespeople is not asking the question.

The second most frequent error is asking it incorrectly. Asking in the following way is a mistake.

(Don't say:) "Are you the decision maker?"

It looks straightforward and simple. What could possibly be wrong, you ask. First, it ignores the reality of how most decisions are made. Most buying decisions, at least buying decisions of any size are made in consultation with others. Only small transactional sales are made by individuals without consultation with others. If your selling situation is retail, transactional, or small sales, you may be able to ignore this play. Otherwise, asking, "are you the decision maker," mistakes the reality of how decisions are made.

The second error of asking, "Are you the decision maker?" is you back the buyer into an ego corner. You have invested careful thought into crafting and executing Plays that build trust and relationship and then you risk invalidating the buyer, eroding the relationship and offending the process.

When you ask, "Are you the buyer?" it leaves the target of your question with no good answer. It's likely that he is not the sole decision maker but that he is part of the decision-making process. The seller's question called for a "yes," or a "no" answer. Neither answer is exactly right. A "no" answer is tantamount to saying, "I'm a fraud. I've been pretending to be an important person, but really, I'm so insignificant that I can't even make simple decisions."

Few buyers are consciously aware of the emotional tug-or-war that goes on in this situation. Nevertheless, faced with the possibility of an emotionally debilitating "No," buyers often just say, "Yes." Their answer is not intended to mislead or deceive. They are, in fact, charged to gather facts and make some initial decisions although, in the end, they may not be the sole decision maker. Now the problem is that the sales process is isolated from the people who will eventually have to weigh in. Getting ink on paper is now much more difficult. When a single individual declares that he is the decision maker, the decision he can make without any permission is "No."

Getting this play wrong is very easy. The good news is that getting it correct is equally simple. Here are some excellent examples of how to run the decision-making play.

"How are buying decisions made inside your firm?"

"Who do you usually consult on decisions like this?"

"What is the decision-making process?"

As the buyer describes the process make sure to carefully record the flow including the sequence and the people involved. This is important information to a successful sale!

Financial Ability to Pay

Closing a deal may be an issue of timing. For that reason, it is helpful to build urgency in advance of asking the Budget and Financial Ability question. Urgency is developed by following the sales process, running the plays and scheduling the next event. The quality and size of the benefits available to the buyer also influences buyer urgency.

Seasonality, priority targets on projects, a change of personnel or unspent budget dollars are all factors in the Financial Ability to Pay. Sellers can also influence urgency and timing. Here are some examples:

Why is this a good time to be thinking (working on, acting on) this (issue, topic, feature)?

What is the most important aspect or action?

What makes this a priority?

Why is this urgent?

What stimulates you to be thinking about this now?

Why now?

Being aware of obvious and seasonal deadlines will help stimulate urgency. Drilling for non-obvious deadlines can help you create urgency. Leading these questions with a reframe of issues as you understand them will help you avoid land mines of idiocy by ignoring the obvious. Asking the Financial Ability to Pay question can be as simple as:

Tell me about the budget for this project.

What budget bucket will you use for this equipment?

How do the financial advantages available here influence your budget allocation?

Get all query examples in one easy cheatsheet at **griffinhill.com/brilliant**

When organizations create budgets for a new year, they often start this budget-building process 3-6 months prior to the new spending year—or even as much as a full year before. Even fiscally disciplined companies understand that they are not likely to foresee and account for every expenditure during the spending cycle that will follow. Salespeople often need to stimulate creative thinking on the part of the buyer. Helping the buyer think about unused or underused budget categories can help them come up with the funding.

If your product or service saves money or creates additional revenue, your cause will be advanced with questions like:

How will the cost savings generated by implementing this project help with the allocation of budget?

How will the revenue generated here influence the budgeting decision?

If budget is legitimately an issue, but only for the timing of the purchase, make sure you keep the company in your pipeline with a clearly scheduled next event: time, date, place—certain; purpose—mutually understood.

Chapter Sixteen

The Plays: Problem Queries

There are three types of problem queries:

- 5 challenges

- 3 barriers

- 1 breakthrough

The labels for these questions describe their purpose and their substance.

The 5-3-1 pattern is absolute magic. Buyers will reach deep to come up with five challenges, three barriers and a single breakthrough. This pattern is like solving a complex statistical problem of factor analysis. You will be able to discern the biggest issues that create problems for the buyer and it will create discoveries for the buyer as well.

I was working with an entrepreneur whose personal take-home spending money was $1,000,000 each month. We were working through the problem queries when he stopped, having just reached several new discoveries about his business operations, and said, "This is incredibly cathartic. Can we do this once a month?" Brilliant questions have the power of making your buyer think about his responsibilities in new ways and that will stimulate new discoveries!

When I ask the 5 Challenges question, I prefer to treat the question and my buyer with sensitivity and respect. That approach continues to add deposits into the emotional bank account even when asking difficult questions. I usually ask it this way:

"What are the 5 biggest challenges facing your industry?"

Of course, the buyer views his industry through the lens of her own experience. For that reason, the challenges she shares will likely be the ones she is facing. Your drill-down questions can confirm this hypothesis.

Having shared his vision, it is useful to your buyer to help her think critically about it. Asking what barriers stand in the way of achieving her desired outcome will be useful to her and to you. It is likely to create discoveries that will open doors to doing business together.

"What 3 barriers stand between you and your vision of_____?"

Asking the previous Problem Queries sets up this culminating question, the single breakthrough. Asking about 5 challenges and 3 barriers has primed the mind of your buyer for a breakthrough discovery.

"If you could have a single breakthrough, what would it be?"

"If you could choose a single thing that would help you to achieve your goals, what would that be?"

"If there was one thing that would help you get to where you want to go, what would it be?"

The single breakthrough question is also a great question any time you are feeling unsure. It may be used when you are in trouble, at a loss of where to go next or when you feel flummoxed. Other ways to ask this question when you are feeling befuddled include:

"Exactly what will it take to make you happy in this transaction?" (deal, case, situation)

"In the best of all possible worlds, if you could structure a deal any way you would like, how would you design it?"

"Exactly what would you like (our firm) to do for you?"

The Problem Queries are simple and effective. They help stimulate discoveries for both the seller and the buyer. You can master them in seconds and they will provide dividends throughout your career.

Chapter Seventeen

Drill Down

Opportunity Queries help us define if and where there is opportunity. They help build relationship and trust with the buyer. Opportunity and Problem Queries stimulate additional questions that facilitate the guided-discovery process. They stimulate discoveries for both buyer and seller. "Drilling down" or simply "Drill Down" is what we call the pattern of asking additional clarifying questions. Once an area of interest has been identified, we dig beneath the surface to stimulate discovery.

Drill Down in Opportunity Queries is essential to draw out all the pertinent facts. Exploring successes and achievements along with problems, difficulties and dissatisfaction is the role of drill-down questions.

Is this function difficult for operators to perform?

Are you worried about the performance you get from your old equipment?

In your drill down, explore problems, difficulties, and dissatisfactions. These queries are Drill Down to answers from Status Quo, Vision, likes and frustration questions.

Drill Down in Opportunity and Problem queries is essential to draw out all the pertinent facts. Open-ended questions will facilitate the drill down.

- what happened

- when

- what was the impact

- how did you deal with it

- what did you say

- how did that go over

- where does that leave you

Using drill-down queries not only fills in valuable information, it gives you a chance to let the buyer dwell on issues, challenges, problems, and barriers. Marinating in the problems for just a bit allows the realities to sink it. When the realities sink in, it can stimulate discoveries and an "eager want" for delivery and protection that you can provide. Let the buyer wallow in the problem and its associated pain for just a little bit while you drill down.

Remember, the purpose of drill-down questions is to secure deeper understanding about a particular point of discussion. Often, exploring these topics more deeply will stimulate discovery for both buyer and seller. The most fundamental drill-down queries might look like this:

Tell me more.

Help me to understand.

Can you explain that in more detail?

Chapter Eighteen

The Plays: Effects Queries—A Special Kind of Drill Down

Effects Queries

We have introduced four categories of Brilliant Questions: Opportunity Queries, Problem Queries, Effects Queries, and Consequence Queries. Opportunity Queries and Problem Queries are primarily intended to help you discover where to focus attention—the X on the treasure map. In addition, they help you discover information that will help you build a compelling solution and proposal.

Opportunity and Problem queries are brilliant because they illuminate discoveries of discontent in your buyer. When your buyer's response provides evidence of dissatisfaction, they have helped you to discover the X on the map that marks the location of the treasure. Buyers may use words like restriction, inadequacy, barrier, dissatisfaction, or unhappiness. To the master salesperson, these are code words for "DIG HERE!"

Here are some examples of language that, when used by buyers, signal dissatisfaction with the status quo. Responses like these help master sellers to know where to drill down.

Our present system can't process the material fast enough.

Lengthy quality control procedures get in the way of delivering satisfied customers. They add weeks to delivery without reducing error.

I'm unhappy about the amount of time we waste in our current process.

We're not satisfied with our current speed. Our customers are demanding more and so are we.

We're wasting too much time and money in equipment maintenance.

We're looking for system redundancy. Without backup we're at risk.

How would that help?

Why is it important to solve this problem?

Effects Queries and Consequence Queries have the additional and distinct role of helping buyers to discover, for themselves, that they need and want a better solution. The queries develop dissatisfaction into formidable fortresses of need and eager want. Eager want becomes intention to act and commitment to buy.

When sellers hear language from buyers that contains a hint of dissatisfaction, it is easy for sellers to assume they will win the business. Sellers mistake the shadow of disappointment with a

Discovery occurs when the buyer vocalizes the positive effects of the seller's solution on him and his organization

fully developed eager want and intent to buy. They stop listening and start selling in earnest. The master salesperson exercises just a little more patience. She asks a few more questions and helps the buyer discover the need for a new solution.

Buyer (in response to an opportunity or problem query): Our present system can't process the material fast enough.

Seller (effects query): If you stick to your current process what will be the effect on lost opportunity from slow material processing?

Buyer: I'm not really sure. We could miss out on as much as 30% additional business. So yeah, if there were a way to capture that additional 30%, I would really want it.

We just witnessed the moment of discovery! Discovery occurs when the buyer vocalizes the positive effects of the seller's solution on him and his organization. The buyer discovers both need and want. Shadows of discontent become intentions to act. Even so, we are still a step away from developing an eager want or a commitment to buy, but we are on the right path! In the next chapter, you will see how Consequence Queries complete the job started by Effects Queries.

Effects questions are a powerful way to stimulate a discovery of negative results that may occur if unfavorable conditions are allowed to persist. In the following example, the buyer responds to the 3 Frustrations Opportunity Query. The seller recognizes dissatisfaction with the status quo and begins to drill down to develop opportunities for mutual discovery. The drill-down procedure continues with Effects Queries.

Buyer: We're not satisfied with our current speed. Our customers are demanding more and so are we.

Seller (Drill Down Statement on 3 Frustrations Status Quo query): It sounds like you have had some negative feedback from customers as a result of current performance. Tell me more about that.

Buyer: Yeah. I think we've had more complaints in the last six months than in the last six years.

Seller (Drill Down Statement): That must add to the stress levels for everyone.

Buyer: It really does. Everyone is tense.

Seller (Effect Query): Have you actually lost customers as a result of slow performance speed?

Buyer: We have lost a couple of customers and a half dozen new opportunities.

Seller (Effect Query): If left unresolved, what will be the effect on employee morale, performance, and turnover?

Buyer: We will surely lose more employees. We have already lost some of our best talent.

Moment of Discovery! Shadows of dissatisfaction are becoming intent to act. The buyer recognizes her need and that need is blossoming into want—the intent to act is becoming evident. Consequence Queries will bring us home with an epiphany of value and a commitment to buy!

Effects queries stimulate discovery, understanding and meaning in both buyer and seller. They represent purposeful drill down on statements made by the buyer:

How would this problem affect your future profitability?

What effect does this reject rate have on customer satisfaction?

What would be the effect of speeding up this process by 10 percent?

If we could improve the quality, how would that help you?

Why is it important to solve this problem?

What benefits do you see?

What bothers you about this?

I sense you are frustrated by _____.

How difficult a spot does that place you in?

One helpful technique is to restate expressed dissatisfaction around quality, production quantity, difficulty of use, maintenance costs, age, training costs and turnover issues. After restating the dissatisfaction, ask about the effects of the condition that causes the dissatisfaction.

You say your equipment is costly to maintain.

What is the cost in terms of parts and labor?

What is the cost in terms of out of service time and opportunity costs? (How much down-time? What could have been produced during that time by a fully functioning piece of equipment)?

How much are maintenance costs likely to increase?

To what degree will maintenance costs retard your ability to grow?

Not all buyers are the same. Economic buyers, technological buyers, and buyers that will use the product or service you sell are each motivated by benefits unique to their circumstances. Different levels of management are motivated by different factors. Match drill-down questions to the motivations associated with the level of management and decision-making authority of the buyer with whom you are speaking. If your buyer has profit/loss responsibility, then Profit benefits will motivate him. Help him to discover your ability to cut costs or increase profitability.

For buyers with profit/loss responsibility, questions that look like this will be helpful:

What if we reduced your per-unit cost by 30%? What would that do for your organization? (Testing my hypothesis of increasing units produced each hour. Effectively cutting the wage cost per unit—my hypothesis is we can produce units faster with fewer errors using her equipment.)

What is the effect of that (negative condition) on productivity?

What is the effect of the (negative situation) on revenue? Costs? Vision (IPO)?

Status Quo Drill Down on how many units are they producing:

How does that compare with expectations?

What if we could increase 30% with no loss of quality? What would be the effect on cost?

What would be the result if we could reduce per unit cost by 30%?

Prestige and Pain Relief benefits are perfect to motivate front line supervisors and managers. When you have front line managers as your buyer you should be prepared with questions like:

How is that working out for you in terms of reaching your desired results?

To what degree is that approach motivating the target behavior?

How are results stacking up against expectations?

What would happen if we tried ____ (new proposed solution)?

If we implemented this strategy where would that take us?

If you could design the solution (deal, transaction) any way you like, what would it look like?

How would ____ (seller's feature based on issue discovered in SQ) help you?

Why would this feature be of benefit to you?

If we could do____ for you what effect would that have on ____?

Here is a role play scenario for a seller representing a manufacturing equipment supplier.

Scenario—Seller represents a manufacturing equipment supplier. Seller has an appointment with a prospect currently using a competitor's equipment. In six steps of planning, seller sets her goal: to stimulate, in the prospect, a discovery that what they are doing today is inadequate and that there is a better path. In seller's research, she discovers that the prospect is using the PX10 model of her competitor. Because she knows her own product's strengths relative to her competitor's PX10, she prepares and executes the following Needs Audit sequence. We pick up the action after the seller has confirmed the accuracy of her facts and hypotheses using Opportunity Queries and Problem Queries.

Remember that the "Opportunity Queries" and "Problem Queries" establish rapport and build relationship. They establish positive deposits in the emotional bank account. The leading statement below is too jolting for "Opportunity Queries", but by the time we get to "Effects" and "Consequence" Queries, trust and relationship are well established and buyer and seller are engaged in a fact based and professional conversation.

Seller (Leading Statement, Drill Down Query): You have probably read the same article that I read in the "Manufacturing Today" magazine. The article claims that high error rate increases frustration of operators. It also reports that the PX10, the equipment you're using, has the highest error rate in the industry. If the author is correct, it would predict morale issues among your team. Tell me about the current morale of your operators.

Buyer: You nailed it. They are frustrated. They complain and murmur all the time. They inappropriately express anger. An unacceptable number of employees show up late for work. Absenteeism is too high and my turnover rate is excessive. Now that I think about it, our current equipment is eroding morale and doing damage to my people.

Seller (Validate followed by drill down query): Your insight is spot on—showing up late, high absenteeism and complaining are not your fault at all. Your equipment is causing poor performance in your people. Great observation. How much higher than expected is the turnover of your equipment operators?

Buyer: I lose employees every month at a rate 1-2 people higher than expected.

Seller: How long does it take to get a new employee hired and up to speed?

Buyer: It's at least 30 days for training alone.

Moment of discovery! Buyer is beginning to feel dissatisfaction related to excess employee turnover. In the next chapter, we will develop the buyer's dissatisfaction using Consequence Queries. Remember, it is the seller's hypothesis that error rate with the PX10 is high and that error rate contributes to poor employee morale and high turn-over. It is important for the seller to help the buyer discover that connection for herself. Consequence Queries will help us accomplish that goal.

Seller: If we could cut the error rate by 90% what would be the effect on productivity?

Buyer: If we could reduce our error rate by 90%? We would produce an additional 100 units per month.

Seller: How would your people feel about increased productivity with nearly no error rate?

Buyer: Yeah, well, that would definitely boost morale.

The pattern of discovery continues! Answers to the Effects Queries demonstrate that the buyer is making new discoveries. These discoveries tee-up the Consequence Queries as illustrated in the next chapter.

Though we talk about OPEC (Opportunities, Problems, Effects, and Consequence Queries) in that order, it does not mean that you wait to ask Effects and Consequence queries until you are completely through all your Opportunity and Problem queries. Use Opportunity and Problem queries to identify where the treasure is, the X on the treasure map, and then begin to dig or drill down using Effects and Consequences queries to test your hypothesis regarding the location of treasure. You can return to additional Opportunity Queries and Problems Queries if you desire.

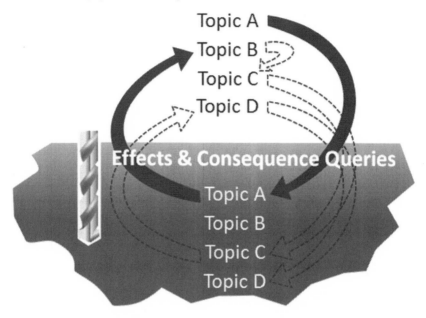

As the illustrations show, you might start with Topic A, do some drill down all the way to Effects and Consequence queries. Once you exhaust Topic A to full benefit discovery, you move on to Topic B, returning to Opportunity Queries. In this example, your O & P queries yield no treasure mark for drill down, so you move on to Topic C. You are able to drill down for both Topics C & D.

Effects Queries are brilliant because they illuminate, for both the seller and the buyer, the need for the seller's solution. Effects Queries identify areas of dissatisfaction. They develop discontent into eager want.

It is not enough to tell a buyer that a deal with you delivers 100% ROI; you must help them to discover it for themselves.

I recently experienced this "discovery of value" phenomenon myself in an unexpected place. On a beautiful fall weekend, I planned to weatherproof my driveway in preparation for the destructive ice and snow of our severe Utah winters. I assembled the list of supplies I needed and drove to my local ACE Hardware store. With my selections made and everything I needed in my basket, I was ready for the register.

The clerk was well trained, friendly and professional and on the alert for an opportunity to sell me additional products. I politely responded that I didn't need any of the amazing and specially priced items he mentioned. In conclusion, he asked if I would like to buy an ACE Hardware T-shirt. Again, I responded with a "No, thank you." He persisted, "If you buy a T-shirt for $5.00, I will give you half off any item in your basket."

> It is not enough to tell a buyer that a deal with you delivers 100% ROI; they must discover it for themselves

The clerk's offer stimulated interest and I quickly evaluated the items in my basket. Each 1-gallon can of driveway sealer was priced around $30.00. The math was not hard.

If I bought a $5.00 T-shirt, the clerk would reduce the price on one gallon of sealer by $15.00. Subtracting the cost of the T-shirt, I would net $10.00—a 200% ROI! I suddenly wondered if I needed a $500.00 tool set. Suppressing my new found eager want, I accepted the offer and exchanged my $5.00 for a T-shirt and a $15.00 discount.

My "No thank you" became curiosity and interest. I judged the purchase of the T-shirt to be a "worthy purchase" or to be "worth it." Buying the T-shirt returned real value to me. My Scots-Irish ancestry and penny-pinching nature rapidly turned me from a confirmed "No" to an enthusiastic "Yes." What's more, my only buyer's remorse I experienced was that I didn't restrict my initial purchase to one gallon of concrete sealer and go through the line five more times! After all, doesn't every weekend handyman need six ACE Hardware T-shirts?

In the same way that I discovered the financial reasons to buy an ACE Hardware T-shirt, the unique role of Consequence Queries is to stimulate discovery, in the buyer, of the business case for making the purchase—the value proposition. While motivation to buy can vary for different kinds of buyers—technology buyers are interested in features compared with the latest and greatest technology, users are focused on functionality and ease of use and economic buyers are focused on the financial advantages of making the purchase—at some level there is an economic justification for spending money.

Buyer (in response to an opportunity or problem query): Our present system can't process the material fast enough.

Seller (effects query): If you stick to your current process what will be the effect on lost opportunity from slow material processing?

Buyer: I'm not really sure. We could miss out on as much as 30% additional business.

To this point, the scenario remains the same as in the previous chapter. The seller does a masterful job of using Effects Queries to stimulate a discovery. Even great salespeople often stop at this point believing they have won the business. The master seller asks just a few more questions to stimulate a discovery of value. Discovery of the value proposition creates urgency, solves remaining budget questions and gives the buyer a strong business and economic case for making a purchase decision.

Seller (Reframe, Closed Ended Consequences Query): What I'm hearing you say is, if we could solve the processing speed problem, you believe you could produce and sell 30% more. Did I get that right?

Buyer: That's right!

Seller (Consequence Query): What would a 30% increase in sales do for your organization?

Buyer: It would be huge. We could invest in more productivity, expand marketing, grab more market share and increase returns to our investors.

Seller (Consequence Query): How would that help you to achieve your vision of _____ ? (insert buyer's answer to the previous vision question)

The seller in the scenario above models a powerful way to transition from Effects Queries and execute the Consequence Query. The seller restates the buyer's discovery with clarity—a great example of a Reframe Play combined with a Closed-Ended Consequences Query. The buyer's confirmation is often the real point of discovery—the moment he realizes the importance of what he just said. Following the buyer's discovery with a further Consequence Query helps the buyer to begin to visualize the new reality and what it would be like. Linking that back to the buyer's previously stated vision completes the cycle. It takes just a few more questions to create urgency and reinforce, in the buyer, a determination to act!

Let's return to another example from the previous chapter. In good Socratic fashion, the Effects Queries created a good discussion between buyer and seller. The discussion concluded in the buyer discovering the need for change.

Buyer: We're not satisfied with our current speed. Our customers are demanding more and so are we.

Seller (Drill Down Statement on 3 Frustrations Status Quo query): It sounds like you have had some negative feedback from customers as a result of current performance. Tell me more about that.

Buyer: Yeah. I think we've had more complaints in the last six months than in the last six years.

Seller (Drill Down Statement): That must add to the stress levels for everyone.

Buyer: It really does. Everyone is tense.

Seller: Have you actually lost customers as a result of slow performance speed?

Buyer: We have lost a couple of customers and a half dozen new opportunities

Seller (effects query): If left unresolved, what will be the effect on employee morale, performance and turnover?

Buyer: We will surely lose more employees. We have already lost some of our best talent.

With just a few more questions, the buyer discovers the consequences of losing customers, opportunities and employees.

Seller: And what about the loss of more customers? Will that persist if we don't solve this problem?

Buyer: Undoubtedly so. We're really at risk here.

Seller: If left unresolved where will you be in another six months?

Buyer: If we don't get this solved, and soon, I'm not sure we'll be here in six months.

The great strength of Consequence Queries is that it creates urgency as buyers gain clarity about consequences. Helping buyers think deeper and to consider likely outcomes will strengthen their commitment to act.

Here are some additional examples of consequence queries:

How does that compare with expectations?

What if we could increase 30% with no loss of quality? What effect on cost?

What would be the result if we could reduce per unit cost by 30%?

What would that do to profits?

If we could increase productivity (feature), what would be the effect on per unit costs (advantage)? What would that do to bottom line—(profit benefit)?

Let's return to the equipment sales scenario from the previous chapter.

Seller (Leading Statement, Drill Down Query): You have probably read the same article that I read in the "Manufacturing Today" magazine. The article claims that high error rate increases frustration of operators. It also reports that the PX10, the equipment you're using, has the highest error rate in the industry. If the author is correct, it would predict morale issues among your team. Tell me about the current morale of your operators.

Buyer: You nailed it. They are frustrated. They complain and murmur all the time. They inappropriately express anger. An unacceptable number of employees show up late for work. Absenteeism is too high and my turnover rate is excessive. Now that I think about it, our current equipment is eroding morale and doing damage to my people.

Seller (Validate followed by drill down query): Your insight is spot on—showing up late, high absenteeism and complaining are not your fault at all. Your equipment is causing poor performance in your people. Great observation. How much higher than expected is the turnover of your equipment operators?

Buyer: I lose employees every month at a rate 1-2 people higher than expected.

Seller: How long does it take to get a new employee hired and up to speed?

Buyer: It's at least 30 days for training alone.

Seller (Reframe, Consequences Query): So what I think I'm hearing you say is, you are losing employees at a rate of 1-2 employees higher than normal every month and that it costs you at least one month's salary to replace every employee. Did I get that right?

Buyer: Yes. That's right.

Seller (Drill Down): And you're paying them around $60,000 per year?

Buyer: Maybe a little more than that.

Seller (Reframe, Consequence Query): Check my math here, but if it costs a full month's salary to replace a lost employee and your EXCESS loss is 1-2 EVERY month, that is equivalent to the annual salary of 1-2 employees.

Buyer: You got it.

Seller (Reframe, Consequence Query): So with employer taxes, your cost for excessive turnover related to your current equipment is between $72,000 and $144,000 per year.

Buyer: I didn't even realize, but yeah, that's got to be about right.

There is the moment of discovery for the buyer! The costs of excess employee turnover are huge! And the costs are directly related to the current equipment on the manufacturing floor. The example continues, this time focusing on the connection between error rate and employee morale and turnover.

Seller: If we could cut the error rate by 90% what would be the effect on productivity?

Buyer: If we could reduce our error rate by 90%? We would produce an additional 100 units per month.

Seller: How would your people feel about increased productivity with nearly no error rate?

Buyer: Yeah, well, that would definitely boost morale.

Skillful application of Effects Queries illuminated two new discoveries. First, a 90% reduction in error rate would result in the production of 100 additional units per month. The second discovery is that an improved error rate would boost morale. Let's look at how Consequence Queries develop the discovery of improved morale.

Seller (Validation, Consequence Query): It seems that boosting morale will help with our turnover problem.

Buyer: I think it would.

Seller: How much of the excessive turnover would it solve if we could eliminate the frustration of high error rate and boost morale by being more productive and respected?

Buyer: When I think about it in terms of reducing frustration and increasing respect... that would absolutely solve my turnover problem.

Seller (Validate, Drill Down): Great instincts! All of the research supports what you are saying. What about the late arrival and absenteeism?

Buyer: Reduce it, for sure. In fact, when I think about the increased respect they would enjoy—I think all of my employees would be more engaged. It might not eliminate lateness and absenteeism, but it certainly wouldn't be the problem it is today.

With the connection between equipment, morale and turnover being clear and quantifiable in the mind of the buyer, the seller can turn attention to the positive consequences associated with increased production.

Seller (Validates based on previous statement, Consequence Query): You are spot on. Let me ask you another question. With an extra 100 units per month what would happen to your per-unit cost of production?

Buyer: Production cost would go down by 7-10%!

Seller (Benefit, Validate, Leading Statement, Status Quo): Mr. Jones, you are going to be a hero around here. You realize, of course, that if you cut costs by even 5%, all of that 5% goes directly to bottom line! What is your current profit margin?

Buyer: Our margins are very tight. Probably 5-6% is all.

Seller (Reframe, Consequence Query): What you're saying is that in addition to solving the turnover problem, we are going to double profits?!

Buyer: That is really exciting.

Seller: Mr. Jones, what I think I'm hearing you say is by upgrading equipment to top-of-the-line technology that will reduce error rates by 90%, you will be able to cut employee hiring costs by at least $72,000 per year, increase employee morale, and double your profit margin. Did I get that right?

Buyer (in awe): I think you did!

These examples demonstrate the power of Consequence Queries to illuminate the business case for making a purchase. The buyer can now see the positive influence on the quality of work-life and employee morale. Yet, with the Consequence Queries, the discoveries don't end with improved attitudes—there is clear evidence of financial advantages for making the purchase. Consequence Queries are all about the value proposition. That's what makes them brilliant.

Illuminating the value proposition is best accomplished when the buyer discovers for herself the benefits you offer as a seller. Brilliant Consequences Queries stimulate discovery of value.

Stimulating a discovery of value associated with your offering is most important in selling situations that are complex. These selling situations usually include products and services with a higher price tag. It can be argued that Consequences Queries are less important in transactional sales where buyers are likely to make decisions based on features and price. For that reason, it is widely believed that retail salespeople don't need to be skilled with Consequences Queries.

While many, maybe even most, retail sales are transactional—buyers making a selection and taking their purchase to a cash register to complete the sale—it is also true that buyers often need information about product performance, use, and comparative features. A perfect example is my purchase of concrete weather coating at ACE Hardware. A variety of products were available. I needed to understand which of the products was best suited for my need. Furthermore, it is reasonable that a better performing product would command a higher price point. As a buyer, I need to understand the value proposition associated with those products. I rely on the seller to guide me in that decision.

Additionally, some retailers offer products with a relatively high price tag. For the normal consumer, purchasing high end appliances, furniture and automobiles is easier with the guidance of a skilled seller.

Finally, luxury items like high-end jewelry call for skilled salespeople that can guide buyers through the complete process starting with Opportunity Queries and continuing with Problem Queries, Effects Queries and Consequence Queries.

Chapter Twenty

The Plays: SNE and Putting It All Together

Questions are brilliant when they illuminate. Brilliant questions illuminate when they shine a light on the path to a win-win resolution for sellers and buyers. Brilliant questions illuminate when they facilitate discovery on the part of the salesperson that will help them to solve problems for buyers. Brilliant questions illuminate when they stimulate discovery of need and want in buyers as they realize there is opportunity for them to improve, grow, become more productive/more efficient, and be enabled to better accomplish their goals and mission.

> **The quality of our systems determines the nature of our achievement**

The focus of this book is to improve sales skills so that we create more win-win deals—deals that improve enterprise and commerce, deals that improve communities, deals that elevate society. When salespeople are more skilled, all of society benefits.

The sincere student of sales and selling will find in these pages principles, ideas and examples that will transform their personal and economic lives.

The ideas presented here are the result of a study thirty years in the making. Three distinct initiatives influenced the outcome: field research with salespeople, surveys of buyers, and finally, evaluation of the scientific literature related to performance and persuasion. Each of these sources contributed to the power, the form, and the function of a new technology for sales and selling.

This new technology of sales is organized as a systematic whole. In every aspect of our lives, the quality of our systems determines the nature of our achievement. We are all the product of the systems we employ. Improving ourselves and our systems will improve our results.

Brilliant questions are a part of a powerful system for improving salespeople and sales results. The four major components of the system are process, plays, metrics and coaching. Process is the simplest way to parse the problem of how to get a sale. Process is a stepwise approach with six simple steps. Case Open (CO), Needs Audit (NA), Solution Presentation (SP), Adapted Solution (AS), Closing Interaction (CI) and Fulfilment and Follow-up (FF). Brilliant questions are nested in the Needs Audit Routine of the Griffin Hill Sales System.

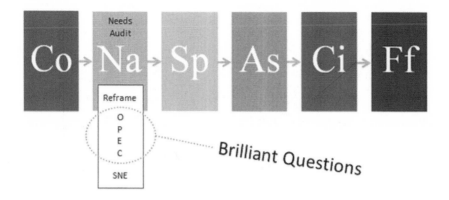

Brilliant questions are Plays. Plays represent principles of thought, persuasion and performance. Plays stack the odds of success in favor of salespeople. Success is defined as advancing the sale and getting more win-win deals—more opportunities, more closes, more revenue. That is exactly what these brilliant questions do. They elevate sales integrity, skill, and results. The patterns you see in this book will transform you and your economic life. You will build better relationships. Serve more customers. Win more closes and earn more commissions as you develop the skill and discipline to execute these plays with skill and integrity.

To help you realize the promise of skill development, we conclude this chapter by modeling several different scenarios using the plays of the Needs Audit Routine. You will see that plays differ from scripts. Plays are flexible in their execution and are customized to fit the personality of the salesperson and the circumstance of the buyer.

The Needs Audit Routine is five basic plays: Reframe, Opportunity Queries, Problem Queries, Effects Queries, and Consequence Queries. The following role play scenarios demonstrate the plays of the Needs Audit Routine. Some scenarios give greater depth than others. Each example is intended to illustrate and exemplify the utility and power of brilliant questions. Each of these scenarios is based on actual selling situations.

Schedule Next Event is a powerful play at the end of every routine. Though we do not explain it much here, you will see it modeled in a variety of ways in the scenario examples below.

Scenario 1—Needs Audit Role Play for HR/Training

Reframe CO:

Seller (Rapport):   Hi Jeff, it's Scott Baird from Griffin Hill. I've really been looking forward to our appointment today.

Buyer: Well thank you. I have been looking forward to it as well.

Seller: Jeff, when we talked the other day I explained that (Positioning) Griffin Hill helps organizations to create well-trained, highly disciplined, and performing teams.

(Benefit) As a result, our clients increase productivity and outperform competitors.

(Proof) I shared the example of iHeart Media. They exceeded their stretch goal by 250% and outpaced competitor profitability by 325%.

(SNE) We agreed that today we would talk about your goals and priorities.

(Opportunity Query—Status Quo) Maybe we could start with you sharing more about your role with XYZ Company and some of your responsibilities.

Listen: Drill Down.

(Opportunity Query—Status Quo) Employee engagement is a big topic these days. What does employee engagement mean to you? What does it mean at XYZ Company?

Listen: Drill Down.

Seller (Opportunity Query—Status Quo): How would you rate the effectiveness of leaders to get employees focused on the most important tasks and keep them engaged?

Buyer: I'm glad we're having a private conversation because you've just hit on something that is of real concern to me. I don't think we have a very engaged work force.

Seller (Opportunity Query—Status Quo): On a scale of 1-10, how would you rate overall employee engagement and productivity at XYZ company?

Buyer: I'd say we're a 5 at best.

Seller (Effects Query): So what you're telling me is that if we could move the needle on engagement and productivity from a 5 to a 7, we would increase the value of our workforce by 40%. Did I get that right?

Buyer: I hadn't thought about it in that way before but, yeah. That's exactly right.

Seller (Drill Down): If we just focus on your front-line employees, what is the average annual salary?

Buyer: We're probably around $60,000.

Seller (Consequence Query—confirmation): That means if we could increase engagement and productivity by 40%, each employee would be worth $24,000 more!

Buyer: Wow. That's pretty incredible. You're exactly right.

Seller (Consequence Query): So if we could increase employee value by $24,000 it would be well worth a $25-per-month investment in each employee?

Buyer: Well, clearly I have to know more but I certainly like what I'm hearing.

Seller (Opportunity Query—Decision Making): Tell me about the decision-making process?

Listen. Drill Down. Record.

Seller (Opportunity Query—Budget): What budget bucket would that come from—employee training and development?

Listen. Drill Down. Record.

Scenario 2—Needs Audit Role Play for Technology Sales

Seller (CO Reframe - Rapport): Mr. Roberts, its Becca Smith with Better Maintenance Technologies. You'll remember that our mutual friend Micah Thomas suggested we get together.

Buyer: Oh, of course. I've got you on my calendar. I was expecting your call.

Seller (Position): Perfect. You'll remember from our conversation last week that we provide our customers with leading-edge facility management technology.

(Benefit): Our technology provides three important benefits—safety, reliability, and reduced labor costs.

(Proof/SNE): We saved Micah's team more than $150,000 per year. I've come prepared to learn more about your situation to see if we can do something similar for you. Maybe we could start with you sharing your role and responsibilities here at FunPark.

Listen. Drill down.

Seller: Tell me more about the connection between maintenance and safety at FunPark.

Listen. Drill down.

Seller (Validate Drill Down): It sounds like safety is the real priority. How many maintenance engineers do you have on staff?

Buyer: We have 30 senior engineers and 10 functional staff.

Seller (Drill Down—Confirming Statement): Wow. That seems like a high ratio of senior engineers compared to functional personnel.

Buyer: We pay a premium for experience. Knowing where all the grease fittings are and the schedule for servicing is fundamental to running a safe park.

Seller (Validate, Drill Down): Makes sense. Are you fully staffed now?

Buyer: I'm fully staffed for the positions I'm allowed, but I could use 10 more full-time employees.

Seller (Drill Down): Sounds like you're stretched pretty thin.

Buyer: Yes. We are. My team is struggling to keep up even with all the overtime.

Seller (Confirmation, Drill Down): Sounds like overtime is a way of life for your team. Tell me more about that.

Buyer: I consistently run 25% overtime in order to get the job done.

Seller (Confirmation Statement, Drill Down): That much overtime can really stretch employees. How is team morale?

Buyer: We pay top dollar so we don't experience much turnover but I worry that my people are exhausted.

Seller (Validation, Drill Down): That kind of mental and physical exhaustion can lead to errors as well as low morale. How concerned are you about mistakes or incomplete work?

Buyer: As I said, safety is our top priority. When work is incomplete or when we risk the safety of our employees and guests, I get concerned.

Seller (Validation, Effects Query): Mr. Roberts, you are right to be concerned. You have a reputation as a careful man. If we could provide a solution that would insure that all your maintenance tasks were completed as scheduled and provide you with all the maintenance reports with a stroke of a computer key, what would that mean to you?

Buyer: That would really give me peace of mind. I would rest easier and undoubtedly my aggravated ulcer would improve—I think my overall health and quality of life would be better.

Seller (Confirmation, Drill Down): Mr. Roberts, you indicated you pay top dollar and your ratio of senior engineers to other maintenance staff is 3/1. For most of our clients, that ratio would be high even if it were reversed. They run about 4-5 maintenance staff for each senior engineer. It seems like your labor costs are high by comparison.

Buyer: That's probably true. That may be the reason that I have an inadequate employee count. More expensive team members means fewer team members.

Seller (Effects Query): What if we created a solution that didn't require the same level of education or experience in the labor force and could deliver superior performance results?

Buyer: That would be huge. I could get more employees for the same dollar amount. That would also help me reduce the overtime.

Seller (Opportunity Query/Effects Query): Mr. Roberts, tell me about the overtime. That has to be expensive. You say you already pay top dollar. Adding overtime must be incredibly costly.

Buyer: Yeah, the bean counters are always busting my chops about it. I get a lot of pressure to eliminate the overtime. But I stand my ground. Our integrity is on the line here.

Seller (Opportunity Query—Status Quo—Drill Down): At what rate do you compensate for overtime.

Buyer: We pay double for our overtime hours.

Seller (Drill Down): What is the average base pay for your senior engineers and maintenance staff.

Buyer: We pay our senior engineers $80,000 and our maintenance staff $50,000.

Seller (Drill Down): And does the 25% overtime affect everyone equally?

Buyer: Yes it does.

Seller (Confirmation): That means your 25% overtime is really 50% more in labor cost. An $80,000 senior engineer is really making an additional $40,000 and maintenance staff are earning an additional $25,000 a year. Did I get that right?

Buyer: You're exactly right.

Seller (Confirmation, Effects Query, Discovery!): Wow. For 30 senior engineers at an additional $40,000 per year that's $1,200,000 in overtime and an additional $250,000 in overtime for staff. If my math is right you're paying $1,450,000 in overtime base. If we add in your employer matching we're well over $1,500,000 in excess labor costs. Did I get that right?

Buyer: You sure did. I've never really stopped to do the math. No wonder the bean counters are upset. That's a lot of money.

Seller (Validation, Consequences Query): That IS a lot of money. If we deliver the kind of solution we've been talking about, we will surely save the costs associated with overtime. But not only that, we're going to get more employees for the same labor budget. Just by cutting back senior engineers to 20 instead of 30, you can shift $800,000 of labor cost to staff roles. That would be 16 more maintenance staffers—that's a net gain of 6 employees. And you would still have the highest ratio of senior engineers to staffers of anyone else in the industry. There's plenty of room for even more efficiency.

Buyer Response

Seller: Listen, Validate and Drill Down.

Seller (Consequences Query): Mr. Roberts, I assume that if we could corral the overtime costs and save your company more than

$1.5 million every year, we wouldn't have any problem getting budget approval for a solution that would cost $350,000 as a one-time fee along with small annual maintenance fee of around $30,000.

Buyer: I could just about guarantee that you wouldn't have any problem getting that approved—assuming we can really save $1.5 million every year without risk of eroding performance or quality.

Seller (Validation, Consequences Statement): Mr. Roberts, based on our conversation, I think you are about to become the biggest hero in the company. We're going to save the company more than $1.5 million, increase your body count, improve efficiency and alleviate the stress on your team associated with the extra hours. Giving you peace of mind and improving your health seems like a pretty reasonable bonus!

(Opportunity Query Budget and Decision Making) It sounds like budget isn't going to be a problem. Tell me about the decision making process.

Listen. Drill down. Record.

SNE

Scenario 3—Needs Audit Role Play Property and Casualty Insurance and Workers Compensation

Seller (Position): Mr. Tenny, we believe it is important to be insurance consultants, not just salespeople.

Seller (Benefit): Our full-service approach reduces the total cost of insurance for our clients.

Seller (Rapport/Proof/SNE): That's exactly what we've done for your friends at XYZ. We have reduced premiums every year for the last 5 years. Maybe we could start by you sharing some of your goals and priorities here at Tenny's.

Listen. Drill down.

Seller (Effects Query. Discovery!): In your last quarterly review with your current agent, what ideas did you talk about to reduce total insurance cost?

Buyer: Well, I'm not sure when we had our last quarterly review and I don't really remember talking about ways to reduce cost.

Seller (Effects Query): How has your "Safety, Security and Maintenance Plan" helped position you with your insurance carrier.

Buyer: Of course, we have policies and procedures. I'm not sure we really have a comprehensive plan. How can such a plan help us with our carrier?

Seller (Response—Positioning Statement, Effects Query): A comprehensive plan helps us to present a full-picture to carriers. It helps us to negotiate better rates as we demonstrate your more disciplined reality. What is your view of a professional and disciplined approach to risk management and insurance?

Buyer: I like what I'm hearing. How much effort does it take from our side?

Seller (Response—Positioning Statement, Effects Query): Our approach to risk management is that we are a team. We provide expertise and guidance and account management to reduce your worry and work. What would it mean to you to have a complete claims management staff available to help reduce your work load?

Buyer: We spend a lot of time on claims management. That could relieve a ton of pressure. That could allow us to focus some of our resources on training initiatives that we just haven't had time for.

Seller (Validation, Drill Down Effects Query): Getting unnecessarily caught up with claims processing can erode productivity on other, more productive issues. How would those training initiatives help the company?

Buyer: Based on the things we have been thinking about we believe we could reduce turnover and improve performance.

Seller (Effects Query): How much do you think you could reduce undesirable turnover?

Buyer: By at least 20%, 6-8 people a year.

Seller (Drill Down): How long does it take to get replacements up to speed?

Buyer: It takes a while. At least 90 days.

Seller (Drill Down): How productive are new employees during that first 90 days?

Buyer: Probably one-third to one-half of expected performance.

Seller (Confirmation, Consequences Query): So if we just take the low end of 6 employees times 3 months, that's 18 months at half productivity means you will save 9 months of productivity cost. At an average employee cost of $70,000, that means you will save more than $60,000 per year in training costs just by utilizing ABC's claims management. How soon would you like to get started on these initiatives?

Buyer: The sooner the better!

Seller (Confirmation, Consequences Query, Opportuntiy— Budget/Decision Making): Well, your renewal is still a few months away. But there is no cost to you to give us a letter of appointment; we could get started on a safety plan as well as working on a claims management system that will alleviate your current burden. How would you like to proceed?

Seller (New Sequence—Effects Query) What does having an advocate to lobby your insurance carriers mean to you in terms of reducing worry and increasing peace of mind?

Buyer: It sounds like you'd really go to work for us. I'm curious to learn more....

Scenario 4—Basic Manufacturing & Equipment Sales

Seller Reframe CO: (Rapport) Mr. Taylor, thank you for meeting today. As you remember from our conversation last week, **(Position) Ulta Machine is a manufacturer of premier widget making equipment. (Benefit) We help improve morale, increase productivity and increase the bottom line. (Proof) That's what we did for ACME Widgets, where we increased profits by 64%.**

Buyer: Wow. That's impressive.

Seller (Validation): We're excited about the positive impact we're having for our customers. I think we can do something similar for you. (SNE) We agreed to meet today to talk about your goals and priorities—is this still a good time?

Buyer: Yes. This is perfect.

Seller (Transition from Case Open to Needs Audit): Mr. Taylor, I've come prepared with some questions that will help me to understand what is important here at Taylor Technologies. I know that time is a premium, shall we jump right into the questions?

Buyer: That would be great.

Seller (Status Quo): First of all, what equipment are you currently using on your fabrication floor.

Buyer: We're using the Altus PX10.

Seller (Status Quo): And how many PX10s do you have?

Buyer: We have 20 of them.

Seller (Status Quo): And how many shifts are you running? One or more?

Buyer: We run two shifts.

Seller (Status Quo): Two shifts. So how many total operators?

Buyer: We should be at around 44 operators to be fully functional. We really need 10% more operators than machines just for back-fill.

Seller (Status Quo—drill down): So you should be at 44, is that where you are?

Buyer: No, we're probably around 36 right now.

Seller (SQ Drill down): 36. Tell me more about that.

Buyer: We're experiencing some turn-over issues right now. We're finding it difficult to get to full capacity.

Seller (Validation, Confirmation): That's got to be challenging. You know Widget Magazine recently did an article on that very topic. You may have seen it.

Buyer: I'm not sure I did.

Seller (Leading Statements with Effects Query): First, they said that high error rate produced by some equipment is creating frustration by operators. In a separate article, they rated the respective error rates and the PX10 had the highest error rate in the industry. With that in mind tell me more about the employee morale issue you're dealing with.

Buyer: It's interesting you use the word frustration. That seems to be exactly what we are confronting now—frustration and complaining seems to be growing.

Seller (Effects Drill Down): Tell me more about the turnover issue. How many are you losing each month?

Buyer: We're losing between 4-6 operators a month.

Seller (Effects Drill Down): 4-6 a month! That sounds high. How does that compare with your turnover rate in other positions here at Taylor Technologies?

Buyer: We would expect to lose less than 1 per month on average.

Seller (Effects Drill Down. Closed-Ended Confirming Question): So among operators your current turnover is 3-5 higher than expected rates. Did I get that right?

Buyer: Yeah. I guess that's right.

Seller (Opportunity Query—StatusQuo): How long does it take to get an operator hired, trained and up to speed.

Buyer: It takes at least a month but it could take 90 days.

Seller (Opportunity Query—Status Quo confirming closed ended question): Industry average for operators is between $45,000-$55,000 a year. I assume you are in that same range.

Buyer: Yeah, that's about right.

Seller (Leading Statement, Confirming Closed Ended Effects Question): Let me just walk through the math here. You're losing—hence needing to hire and train—3-5 more operators than normal because of high turnover. Did I get that right?

Buyer: Yeah. That's right.

Seller (Leading Statement Confirming Closed Ended Consequence Question): Let's just take the lowest end and say 3 new operators to hire and train per month. That's 36 new operators to hire and train every year. Again, if we take the low end of training time—1 month, that's 36 months of excessive training costs. That's like paying 3 full-time operators for a year. Holy mackerel, that's $150,000 a year in excess training costs plus around 30% for matching withholding and minor benefits and that's $195,000 per year! That has to hurt.

Buyer: Wow. I didn't realize it was that much. I've never really stopped to calculate it. That's just scary.

Seller (Validation. Effects Query): You're right! That is scary! I think we can help you to get that $195,000 problem under control. Let me ask a different question. What if we could cut error rate by 90%, what effect would that have on productivity.

Buyer: Wow. That would be nice. Our current error rate is 10%. On 1,000 units/month/operator, we're rejecting 100 units. Cutting error rate by 90% would increase productivity by 90 units per operator every month. On 40 operators that would be 3600 more units per month.

Seller (Effects): If you can produce 3600 more units with the same amount of labor and equipment cost, what effect would that have on your per-unit cost?

Buyer: Yeah. That would be huge.

Seller (Validation, Leading Statement, Effects Query): Mr. Taylor you are exactly right. That is huge. All of that cost reduction drops directly to the bottom line. What kind of an impact would that kind of profitability have on Taylor Technologies?

Buyer: We would definitely be able to accomplish the goals we're currently pursuing. It would also take a lot of pressure off.

Seller: (Validation, Consequence Leading Statement, Opportunity—Status Quo Query) Mr. Taylor, very insightful. You still have material costs but it sounds like we can increase profit margin by 8% or more. What are your current margins.

Buyer: Our total profit margin now is only 12%. Another 8% would be amazing.

Seller (Consequences Query Validation, SNE) You are going to love our solution. I believe we are going to solve your turnover problem and cut $195,000 of unnecessary cost. We're going to cut your error rate by 90% or more, cut your per-unit costs and grow your bottom line profitability by 66%.

Move to Call to Action Close or SNE.

The scenarios are intended to demonstrate a variety of selling situations and application of the principles behind brilliant questions. You may find useful patterns that will guide you as you prepare for your next sales call. Using these scenarios as a regular reference will help you develop greater skill in your chosen profession.

The more competitive the environment, the greater the need for real sales skill

Developing skill as a professional salesperson takes effort. The effort required to be a top sales performer can be likened to an athlete developing their native gifts into professional level talent. Too often, individuals and sales leaders underestimate the need for ongoing development. They mistake native gifts of social skills and charisma as being adequate preparation for the world of professional sales. The more competitive the environment, the greater the need for real sales skill.

Chapter Twenty-One

How to Apply These Principles in Your Very Next Sales Meeting

The plays of the Needs Audit Routine represent principles. The plays are named to easily recall to the mind of the seller the principle it represents. The sequence of the plays is ordered for a smooth interaction between buyer and seller and is based on step-wise principles of human cognition. For that reason, the first step in application is to follow the plays in the designed sequence as you prepare for your sales call.

Tip #1 - Follow the Plays

Reframe	a brief summary of past interactions with a focus on the benefits to the buyer and the agreed upon action or agenda for the current meeting
Opportunity Queries	pairs of questions designed to stimulate discovery of meaningful areas for discussion between buyer and seller

Status Quo Queries	general questions about the buyer's current situation
Vision	questions about goals and desired outcomes
3 Likes	identifies what buyer values and what seller must preserve or expand
3 Frustrations	identifies areas of dissatisfaction and concern
Decision-Making Process	provides a roadmap for getting to "yes"
Ability to Pay	identifies sources of payment and confirms opportunity for a sale

Problem Queries	provides broad opportunity to identify issues that seller could solve

- **5 problems** facing the industry—identifies issues of common buyer and competitors

- **3 barriers** to achieving desired vision—clarifies areas of focus for valuable contribution

- **1 single breakthrough**—prioritizes buyer's perceptions of value

Effects Queries	drill down on possible "what if" scenarios that stimulate mutual discovery
Consequence Queries	drill down that builds the business case for doing business together
Schedule the Next Event	builds urgency to advance the sales process

Following these principles in this order will provide a smooth interaction between buyer and seller that will stimulate mutual discovery of the buyer's needs and wants, the decision making process, and ability to pay.

Tip #2 - Stay focused on the benefits of your product or service

The Needs Audit is an opportunity to test the value of your benefits to the buyer with whom you are meeting. The plays are executed in the context of what you have to offer. To be the most effective, you should develop questions that help both you and the buyer to discover if those benefits are meaningful and useful to the buyer.

To start the process it is important to get the benefits you offer clear in your mind.

Step 1   Ask yourself what benefits you typically promise to suspects and prospects.

Step 2   Consider the benefits claimed in your company's sales and marketing literature or in the materials used for training salespeople.

Step 3   Review customer proofs. Separate from the standard company line, ask yourself what your customers value about your product or service.

Tip #3 - Assemble what you know about your buyer and buyer's company

---

Step 1   Ask what you can hypothesize simply by virtue of the buyer's industry. In what way is the industry thriving? Ask yourself what issues other companies in the industry face. What conditions shed light on the need for or the value of the product or service you offer?

Step 2   What do you know about your suspect or prospect based on publicly available information such as news feeds, websites, and common knowledge?

Step 3   What can you assume about your buyer based on her organizational role and responsibility? Management level influences the kinds of benefits that the buyer will respond to. Users, technological buyers, and economic buyers are each motivated by different benefits.

Tip #4 - Build hypotheses about buyer's interests, needs, wants and motivations.

Decide what you need to discover and what you would like your buyer to discover.

Tip #5 - Ask yourself what queries in each category, opportunity, problem, effects and consequences, will help you to test your hypotheses.

What questions will stimulate discovery in your buyer, of their need and want for your product or service?

These tips provide a practical guideline—a rubric for helping you to create your own brilliant questions.

Get these tips in one handy cheatsheet at **griffinhill.com/brilliant**

These tips will help you to use the plays of the Needs Audit Routine to be a brilliant salesperson. Your skill will elevate your respect with your employer and among your buyers. You will become a trusted problem solver. You will be more skilled, more effective and more successful. You will be brilliant!

This book will help salespeople of all skill levels to transform themselves. It will be transformational for you! I believe in you! You can do this! My whole team is at your disposal. We are committed to help. The Griffin Hill Sales System will help you get more opportunities, more deals and more revenue. It might not launch you into the Inc. 500 Fastest Growing Companies list like it did for IntegraCore, but it will help you to elevate your game with rapid, substantial, and sustainable results.

Dr. Baird and his team are available for live speaking, coaching engagements and consultations. Dr. Baird can be reached at scottb@griffinhill.com. You can reach the Griffin Hill offices at (801) 225-7000 or support@griffinhill.com.

Sources

1. Deseret News Op Ed 8/2017. deseretnews.com/article/865685787 /Boyd-Matheson-If-you-must-speak-ask-a-question.html

2. Overstreet, H.A. 1925. Influencing Human Behavior, New York; W.W. Norton.

3. J.R Stroop. Studies of interference in serial verbal reactions. *Journal of Experimental Psychology*, 18 (1935), pp. 643-662.

4. George Washington: a biography. W Irving - 1994 - Da Capo Press

5. Miller, George A. "The Magic Number Seven, Plus or Minus Two: Some Limits in Our Capacity for Processing Information" *The Psychological Review*, Volume 63, 1956, pp 81-97.

6. Shakespeare. Hamlet, Act 2, scene 2.

7. Erickson, Bonnie & Lind, E & C Johnson, Bruce & O'Barr, William. (1978). Speech Style and Impression Formation in a Court Setting. Journal of Experimental Social Psychology. 14. 266-279. 10.1016/0022-1031(78)90015-X.

8. Anderson, C.A., Lepper, M.R., Ross, L. (1980). Perseverance of social theories: The role of explanation in the persistence of discredited information. *Journal of Personality and Social Psychology*, 39, 1037–1049.

9. Collins, A. M. and Quillian, M. R., "How to Make a Language User", in E. Tulving and W. Donaldson (eds.), *Organization and Memory* , 1972.

10. Loftus, E. F., & Palmer, J. C. (1974). Reconstruction of auto-mobile destruction: An example of the interaction between language and memory. Journal of Verbal Learning and Verbal Behavior, 13, 585-589.

11. Gilbert, T. (1978). *Human competence: Engineering worthy performance.* New York: McGraw-Hill.